OTHER PEOPLE'S
CHILDREN

Other People's
Children

Ben LoPinto

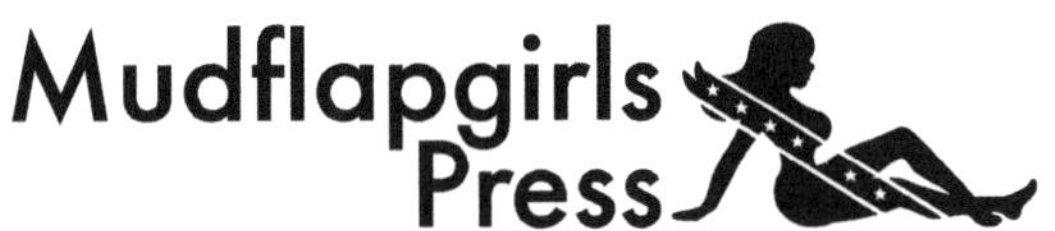

The author wishes to acknowledge Moody's Film Lab in Burien, Washington, for its skillful photofinishing.

Images contained within this book conform to journalism best practices regarding ethics and accuracy, and, as depictions of real events, are genuine in every way. No image has been posed, contrived, or digitally altered (e.g., people or objects added, removed, blurred, distorted, or otherwise obscured) in any way except as described below.

Minor adjustments, which include cropping, dust and scratch removal, conversion into grayscale, and normal toning, are acceptable when limited to those minimally necessary for clear and accurate reproduction of the authentic nature of the photograph.

Copyright © 2025 Ben LoPinto
All photographs © 2025 Ben LoPinto

ISBN: 979-8-9999186-0-4

Library of Congress Control Number: 2025918206

Published in Seattle, Washington, by Mudflapgirls Press.

First edition
Printed and bound in the United States of America.

10 9 8 7 6 5 4 3 2 1

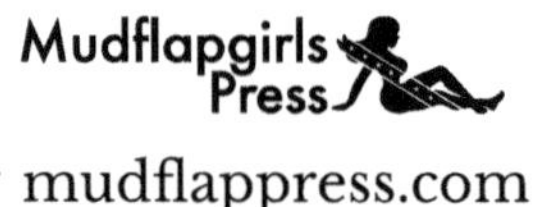

mudflappress.com

"Sharpness is a bourgeois concept."

— Henri Cartier-Bresson

Preface

Getting advice from the internet is like watching a woman shit into her hand. It might start off as interesting, or enticing, or intriguing, but after a moment or two you realize that you're no better off than when you started. If anything, you're worse now for having seen the shit.

Taking pictures of children is among many topics the internet commentariat has strong opinions about, despite kids being one of the top five most popular subjects to photograph and share (along with sunsets, pets, food, and selfies).

Common sentiment among social media users and forum posters trends toward advising curious photographers that they must never take pictures of children in public, even their own, without explicit affirmative consent from the child, the parents, and anyone else who's present.

"It's unethical!" the commentors cry out. "No homeless, no people having mental breakdowns, and no children, ever!"

Of course, this advice is preposterous. What dad wouldn't want to photograph his daughter? What mother doesn't have albums full of her son's baby pictures?

Whose grandparents wouldn't love to display photos of their grandkids on their walls and around their homes, proudly showing them off to visitors?

Alternatively, think about how many newborn pictures have been shared to group chats, or how many "look at my kid making a funny face" snapshots have been shared on social media. You'll find the number to be countless.

Beyond the internet, authors have written countless pages about taking pictures of children. If you pick up just about any "how to take better pictures" book from the past 60 years, you're bound to find a chapter dedicated to techniques and special considerations for photographing children in both impromptu and formal posed situations.

One constant refrain from all of these books, however, is the assumption the photographer is known by the parents or has some relationship with the child.

I know none of these children, nor any of their parents. I had no interaction with them before or after taking their picture. No permission given, no consent sought.

Please enjoy the following
candid, nonconsensual photographs of
other people's children.

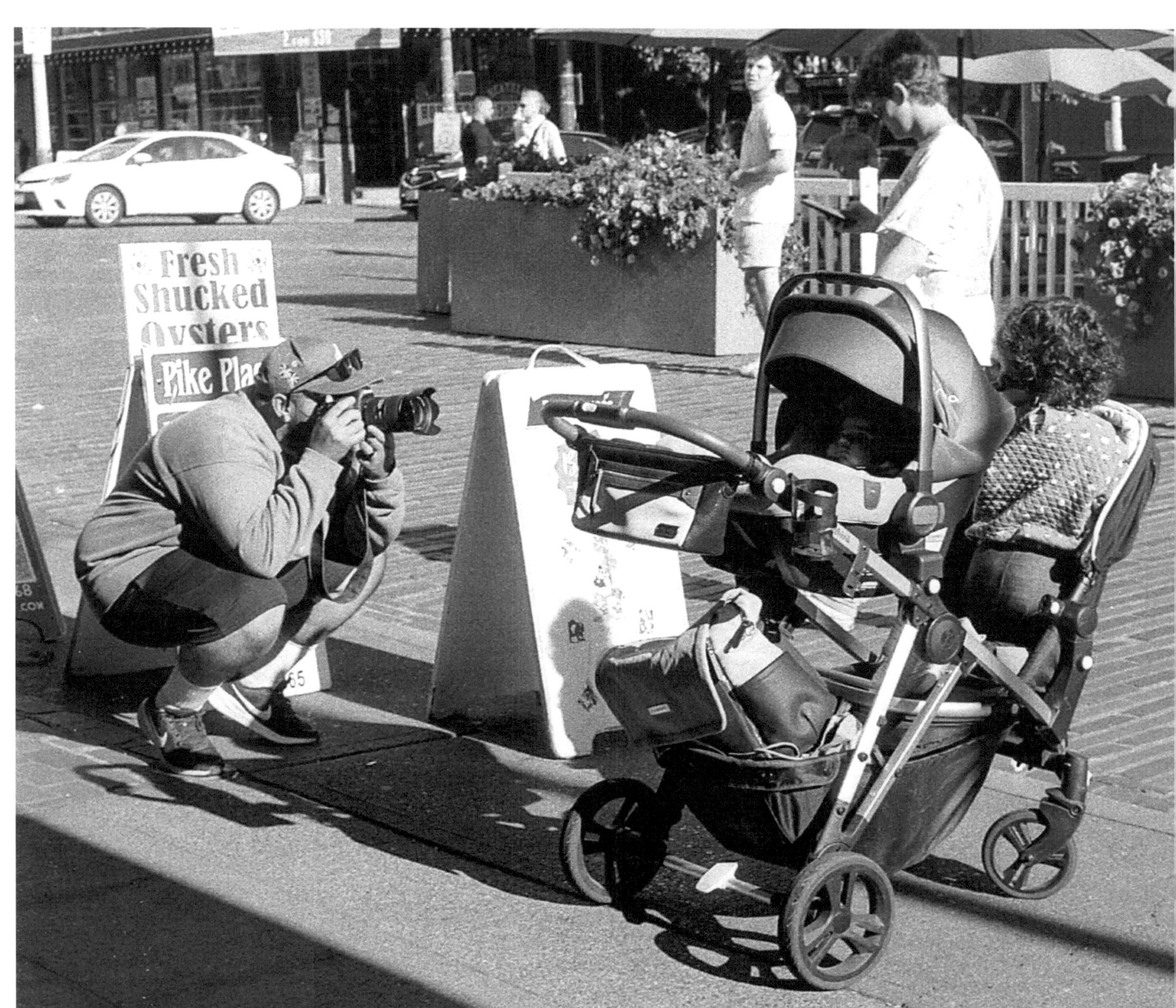

Fresh
Shucked
Oysters
Pike Place

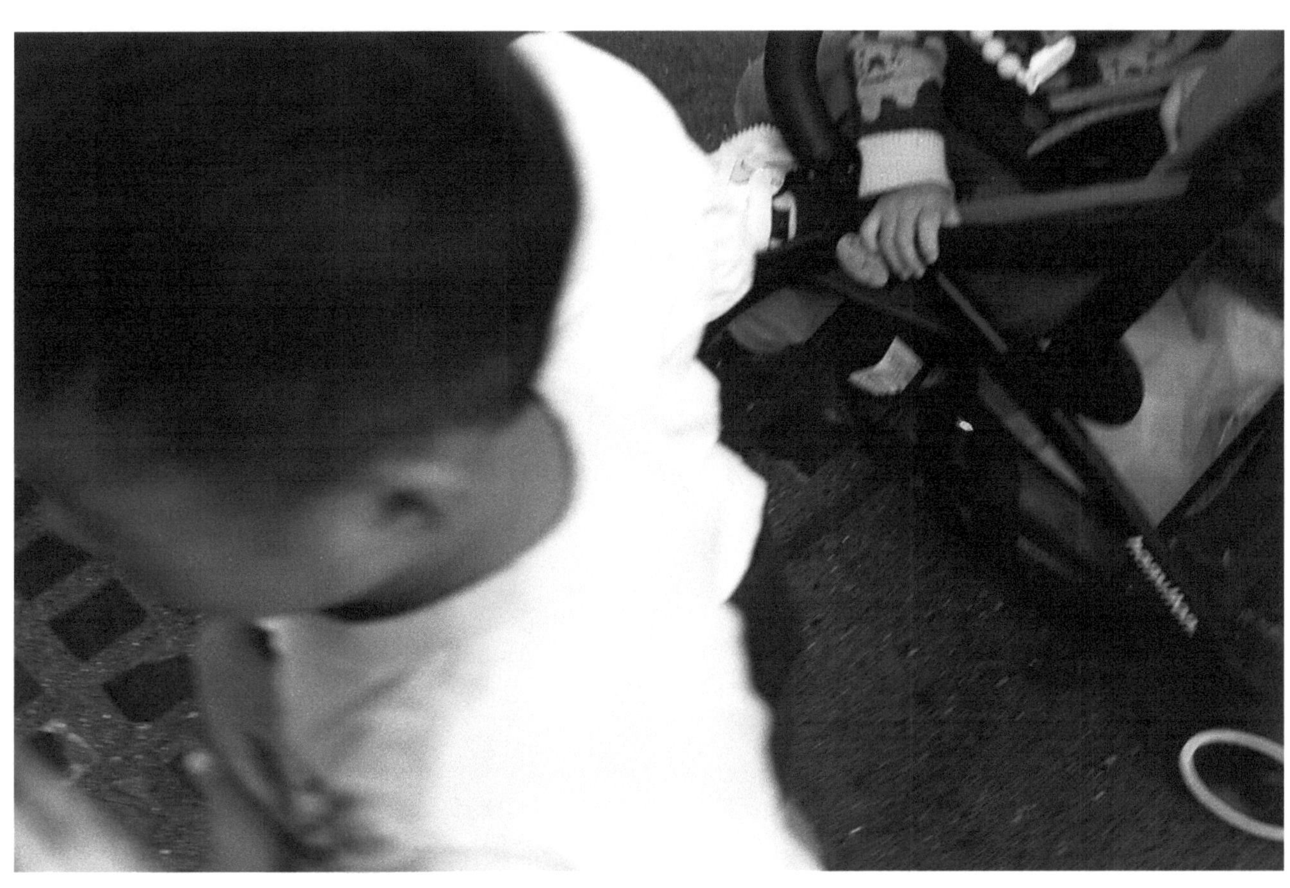

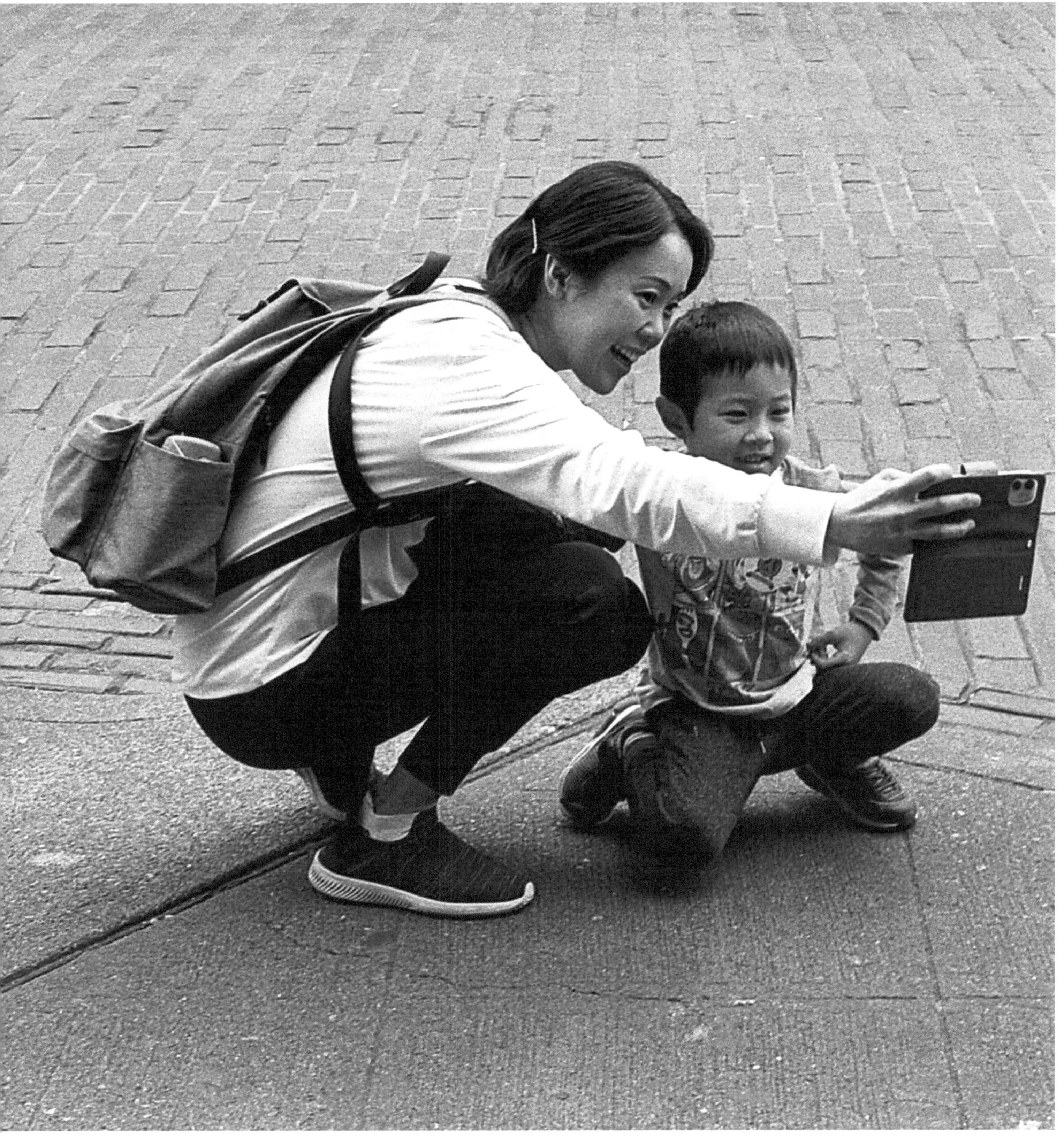

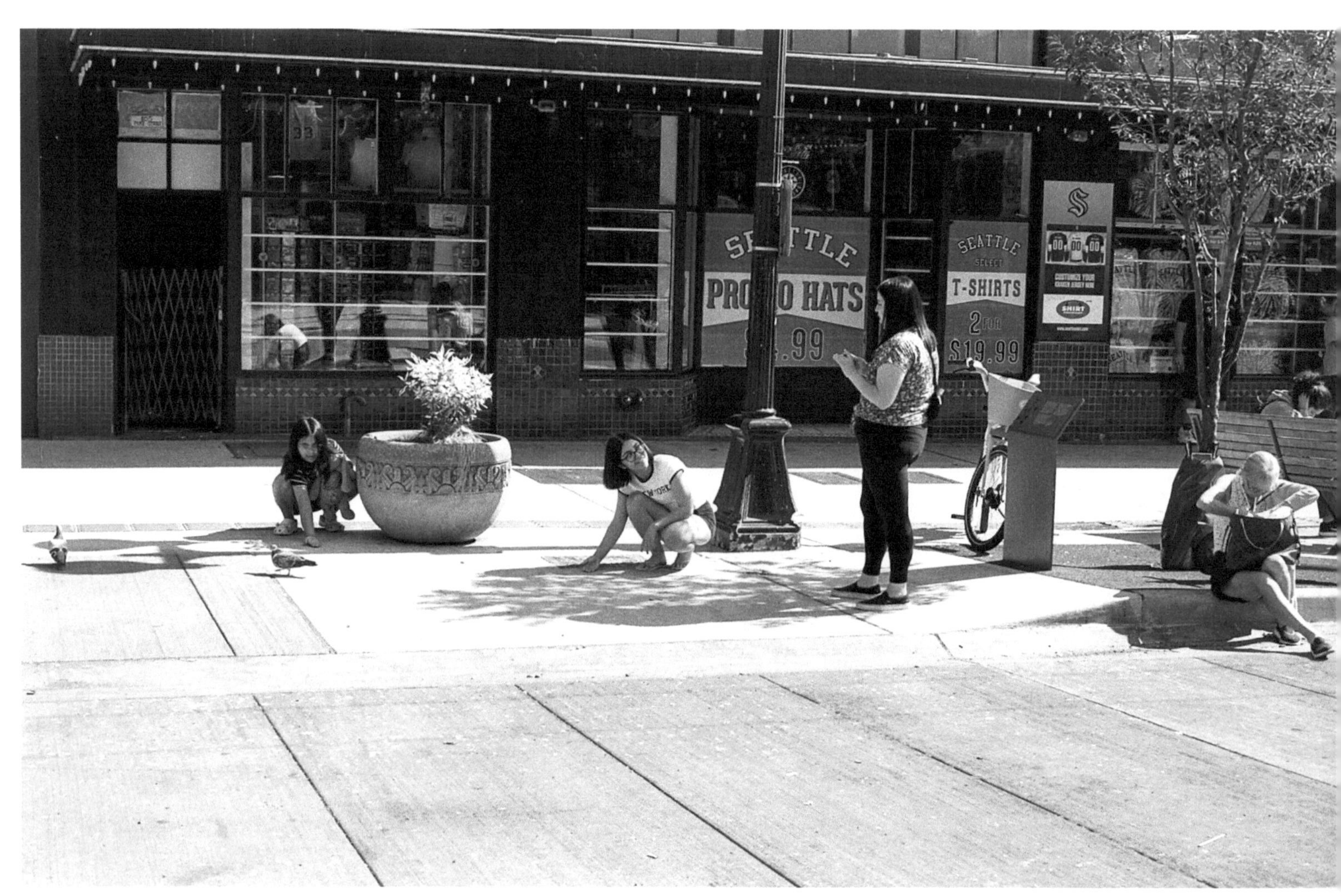
SEATTLE
PRO HATS
.99
SEATTLE
SELECT
T-SHIRTS
2 FOR
$19.99

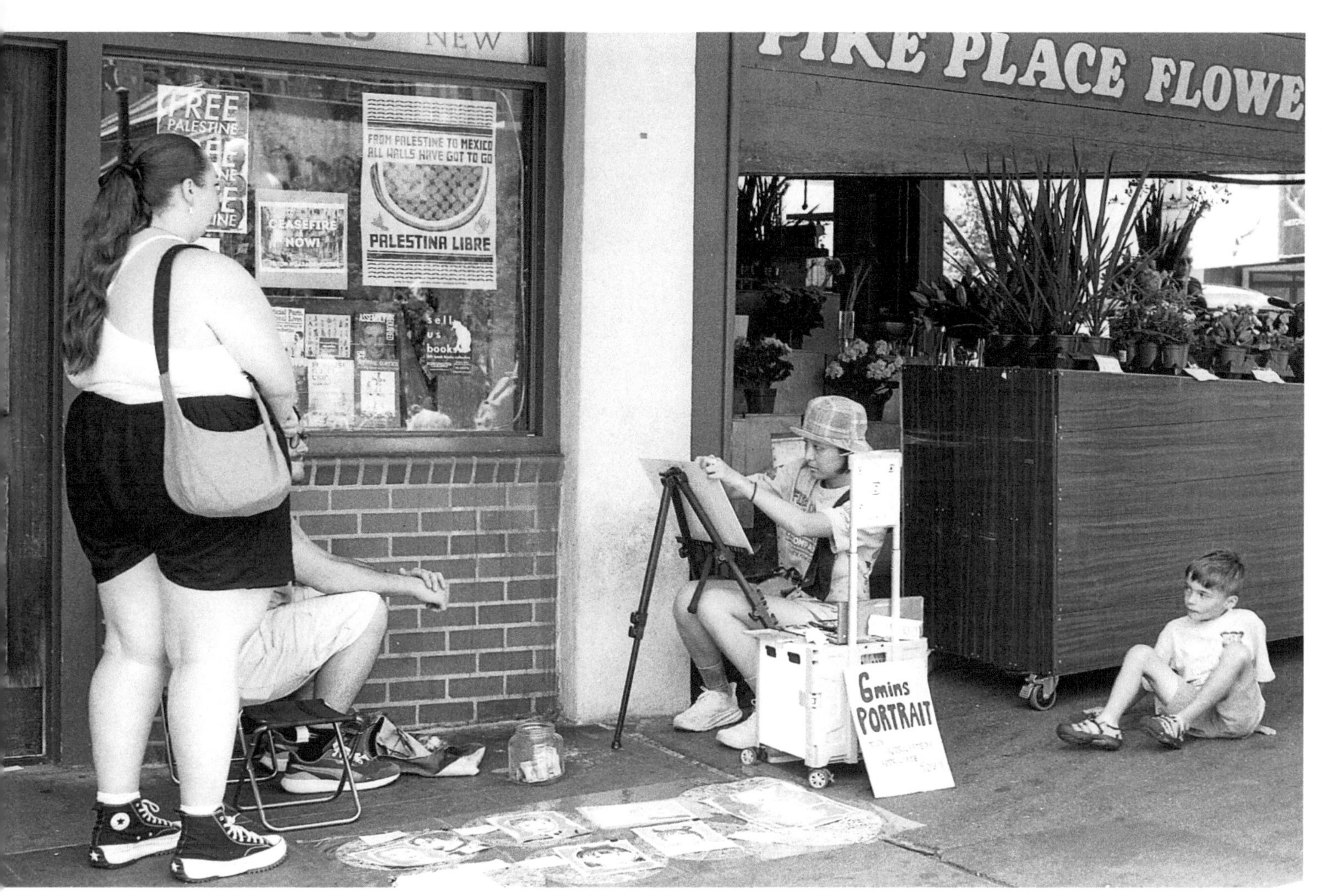
NEW
PIKE PLACE FLOWE
FREE
PALESTINE
CEASEFIRE
NOW!
FROM PALESTINE TO MEXICO
ALL WALLS HAVE GOT TO GO
PALESTINA LIBRE
Sell
us
books
6mins
PORTRAIT

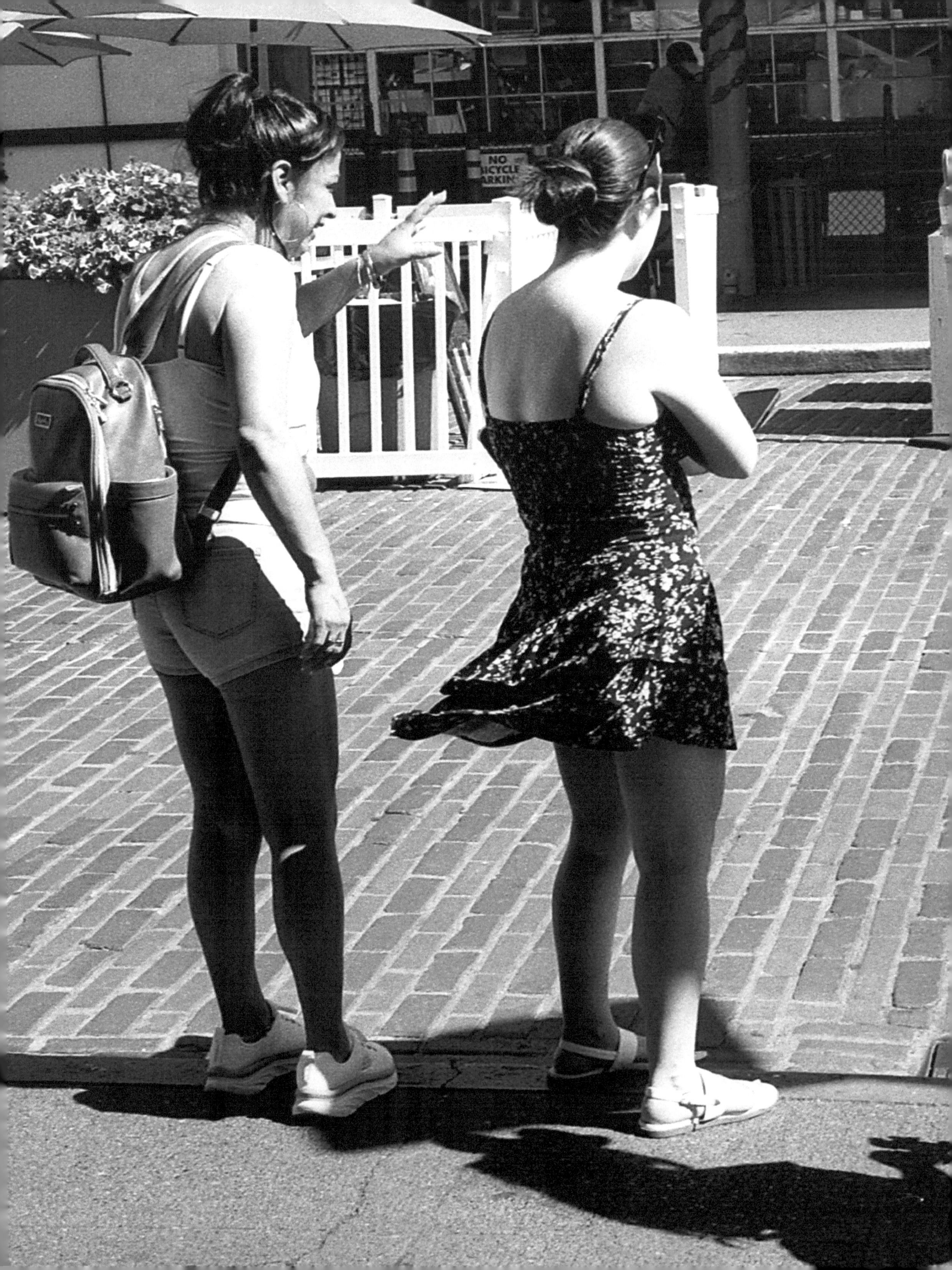

NO
BICYCLE
PARKING

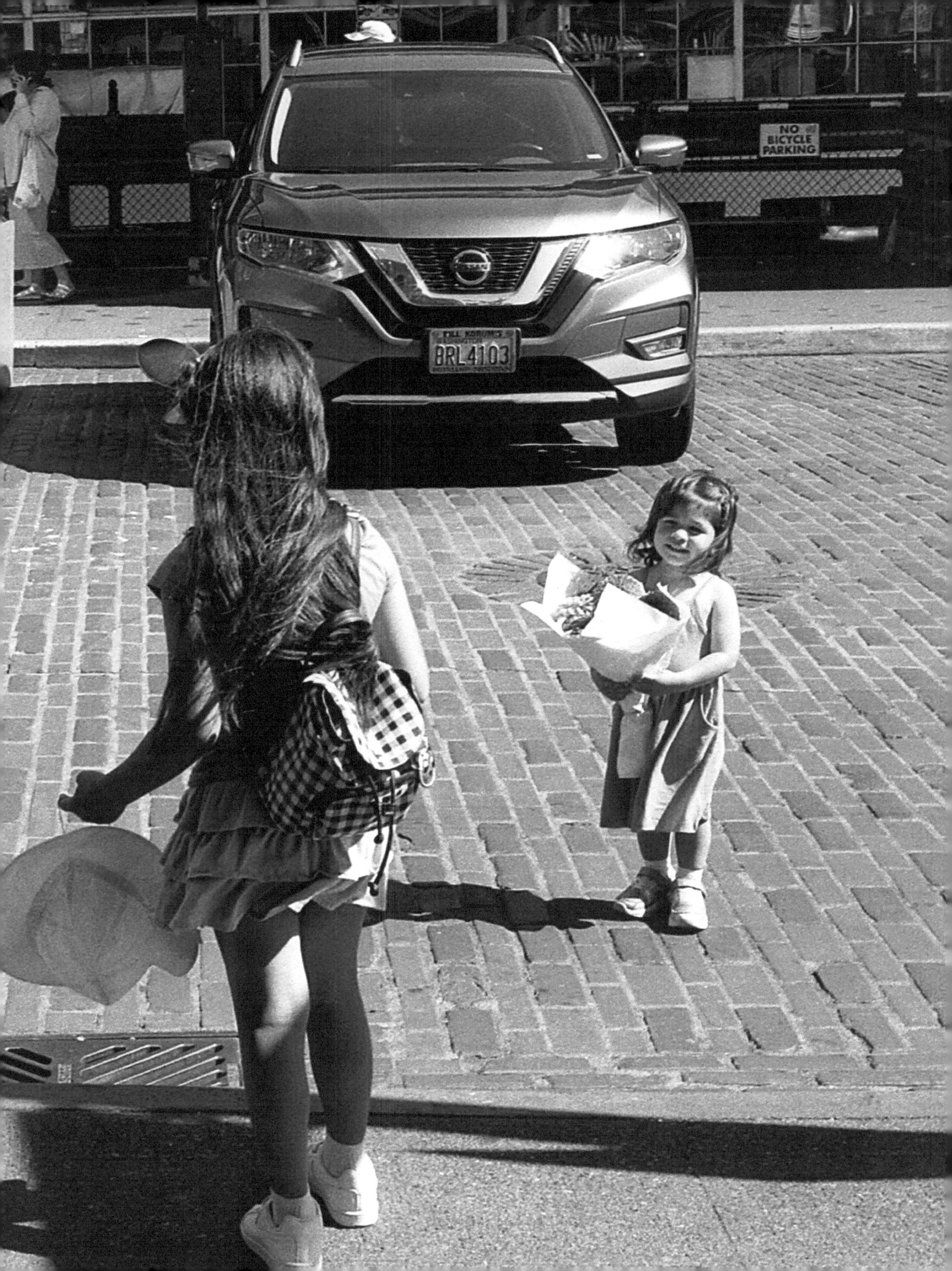

NO
BICYCLE
PARKING
BRL 4103

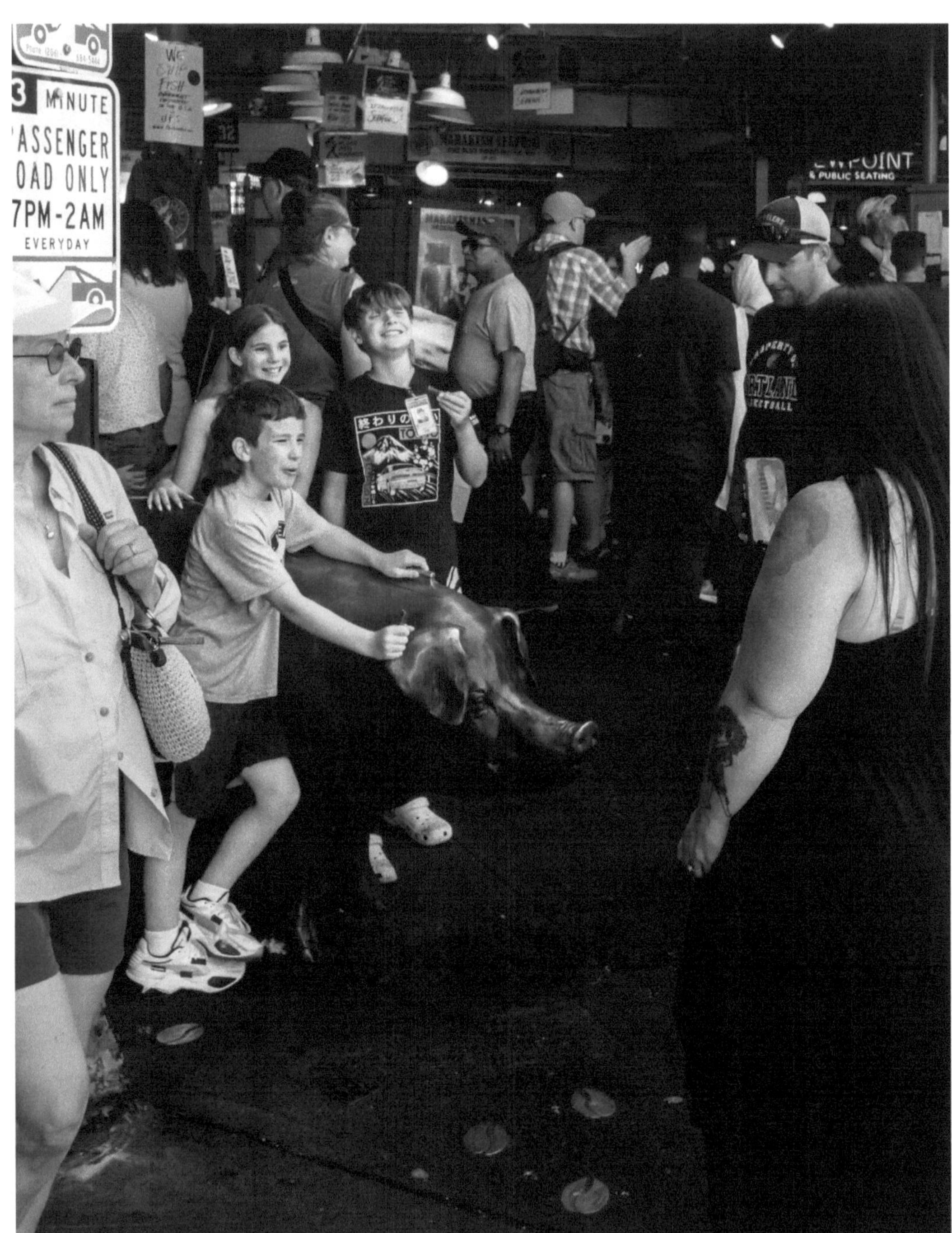
3 MINUTE
PASSENGER
LOAD ONLY
7PM-2AM
EVERYDAY
POINT
& PUBLIC SEATING

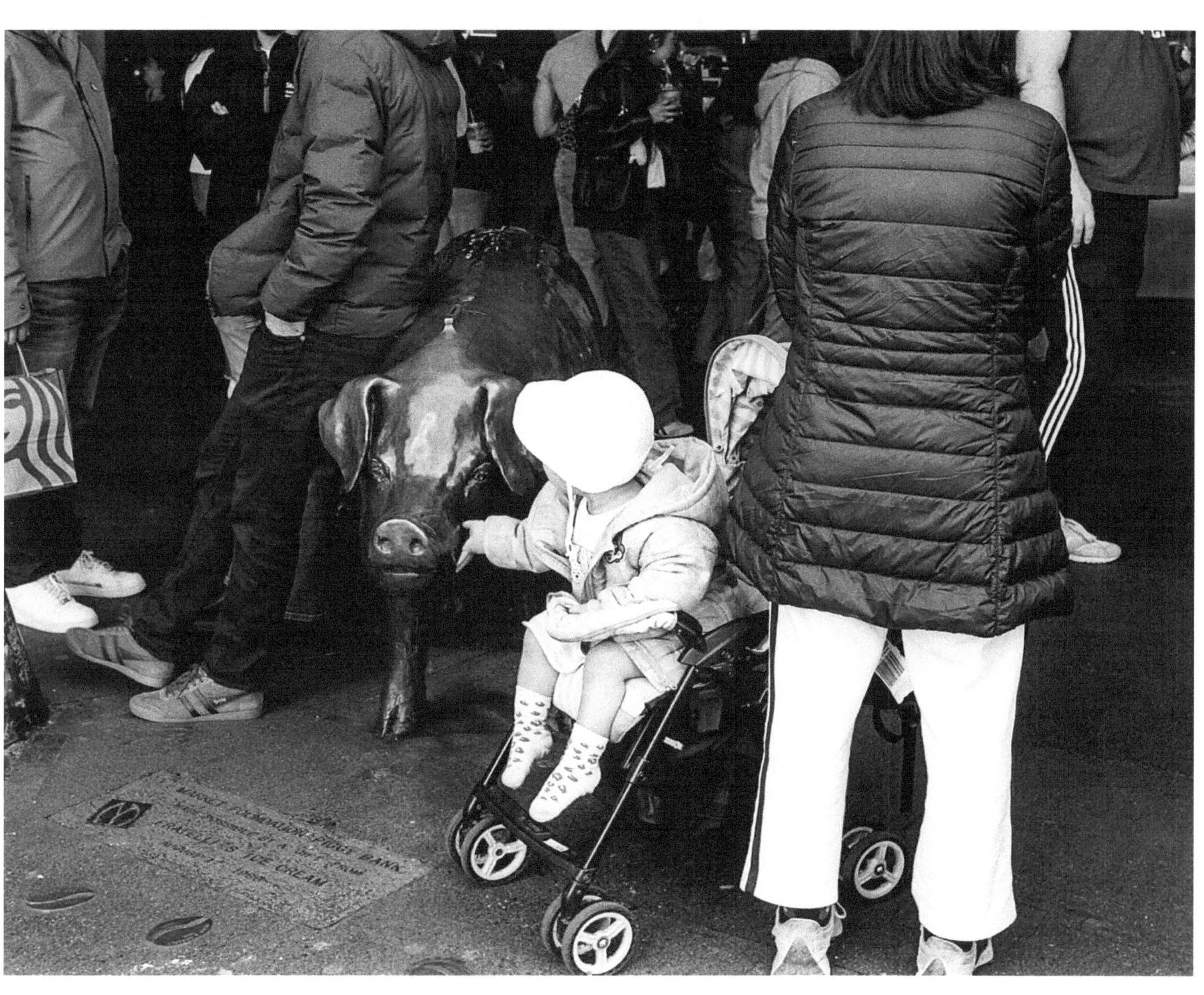

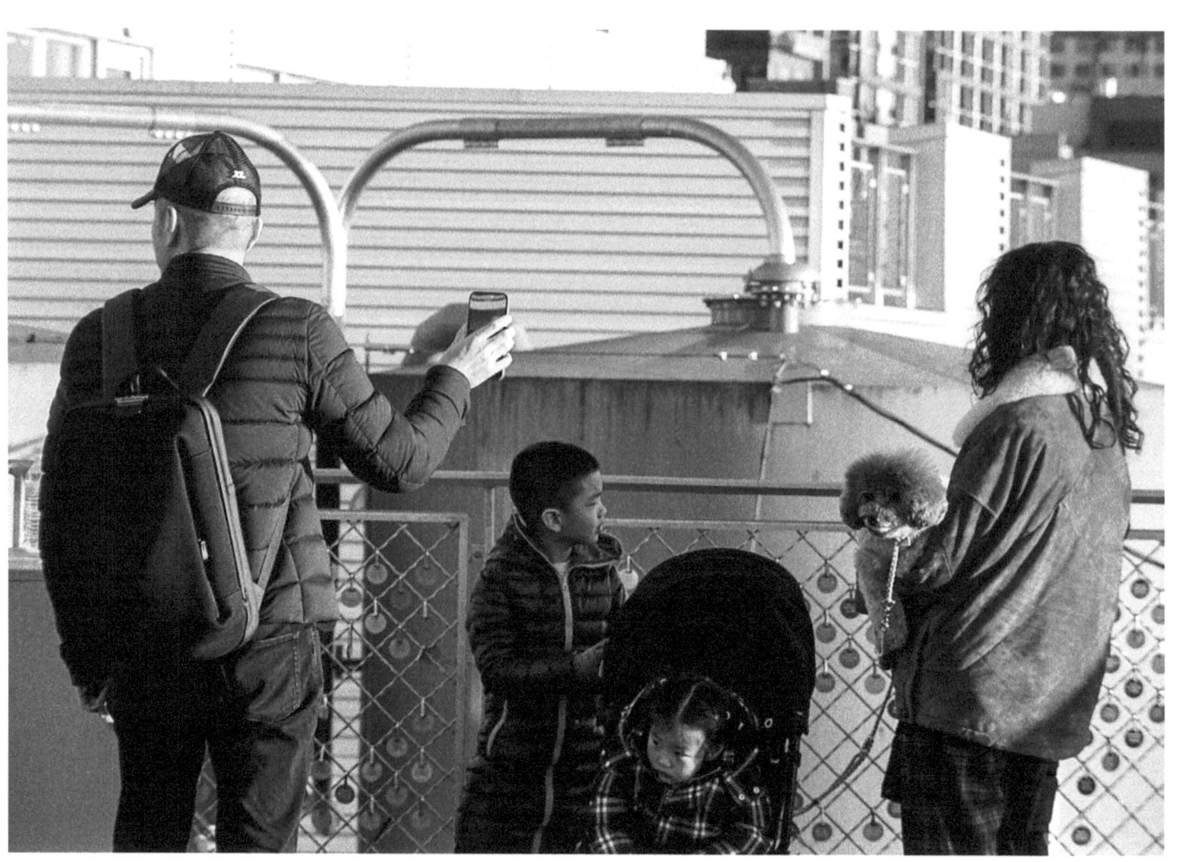

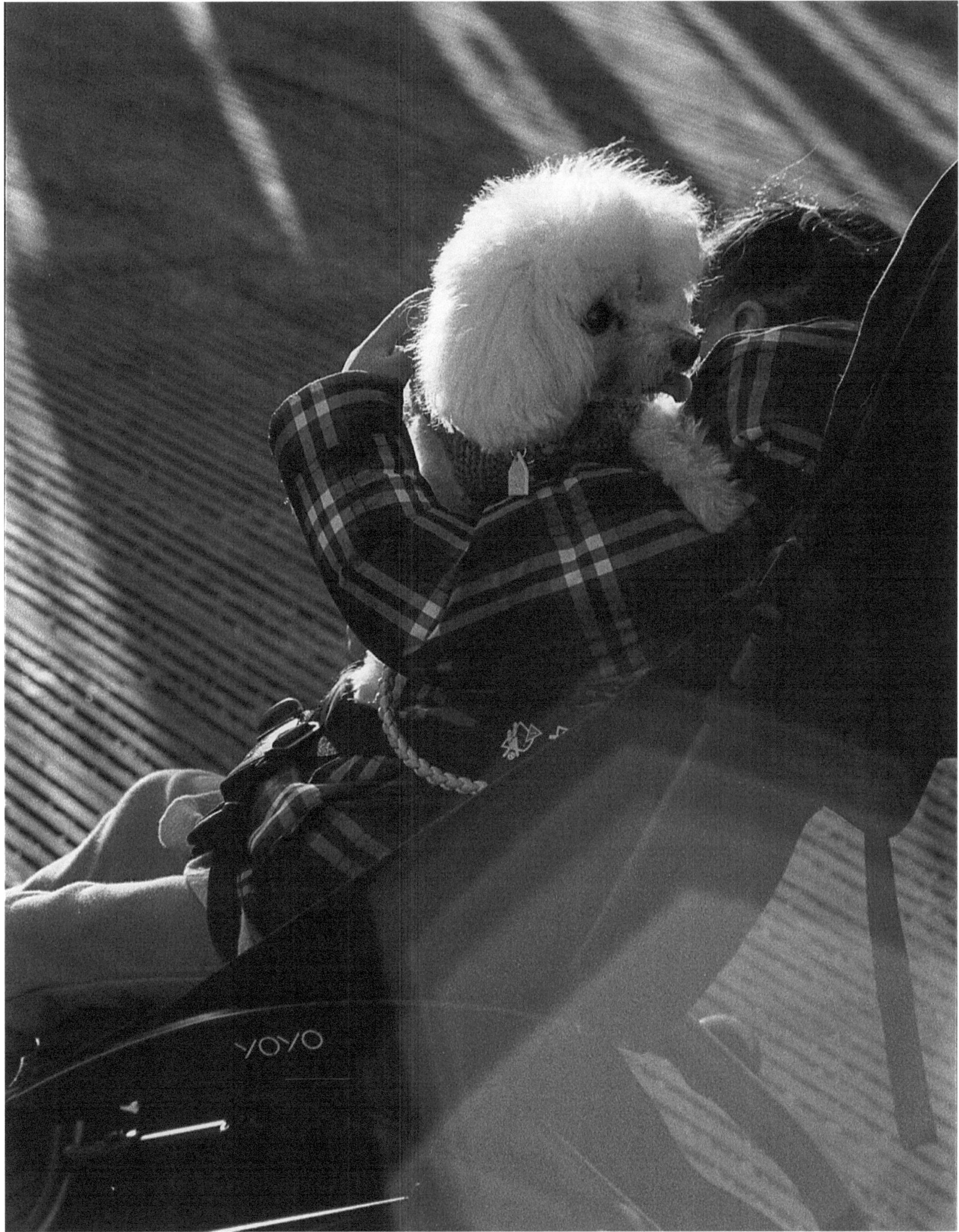
YOYO

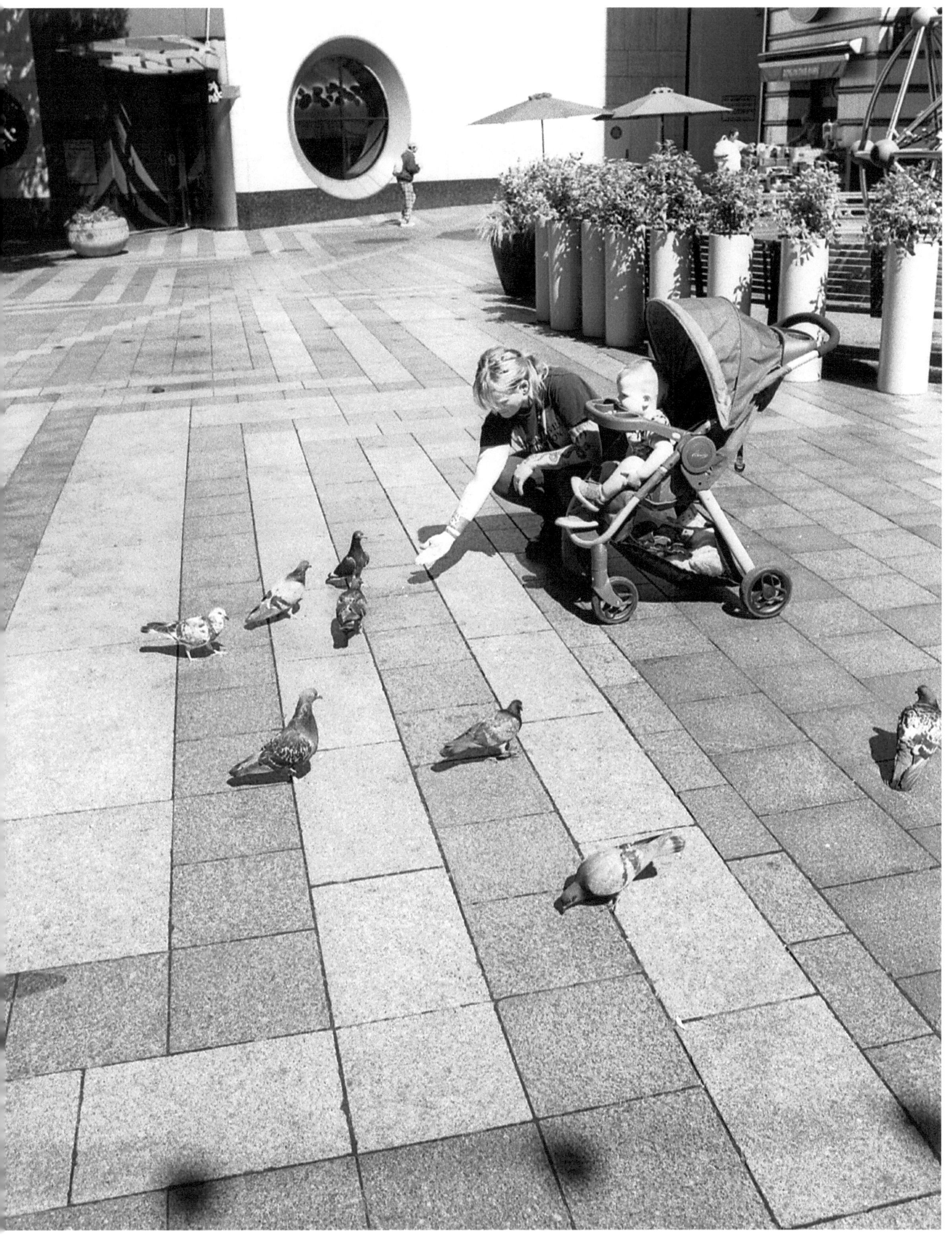

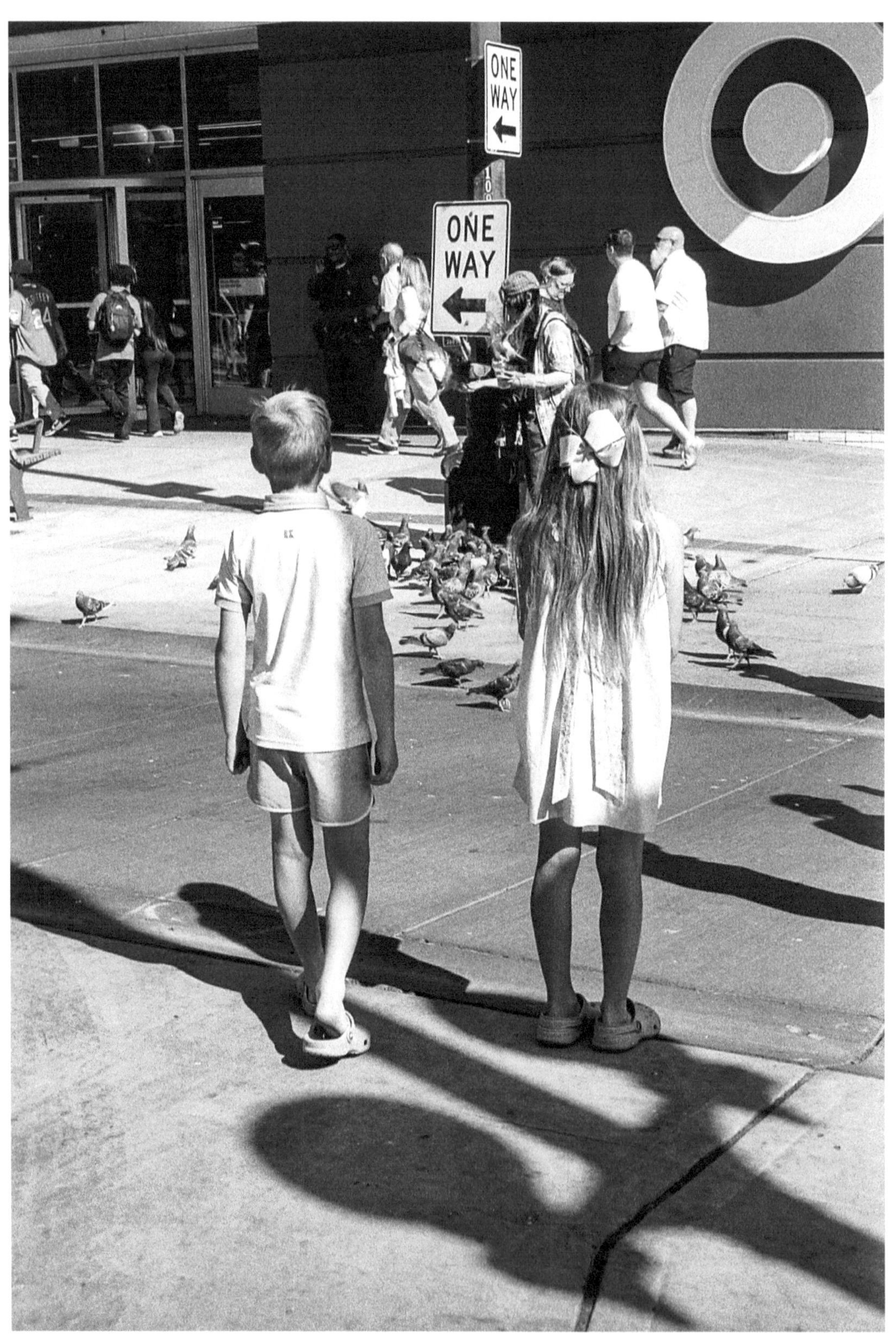

ONE
WAY
ONE
WAY

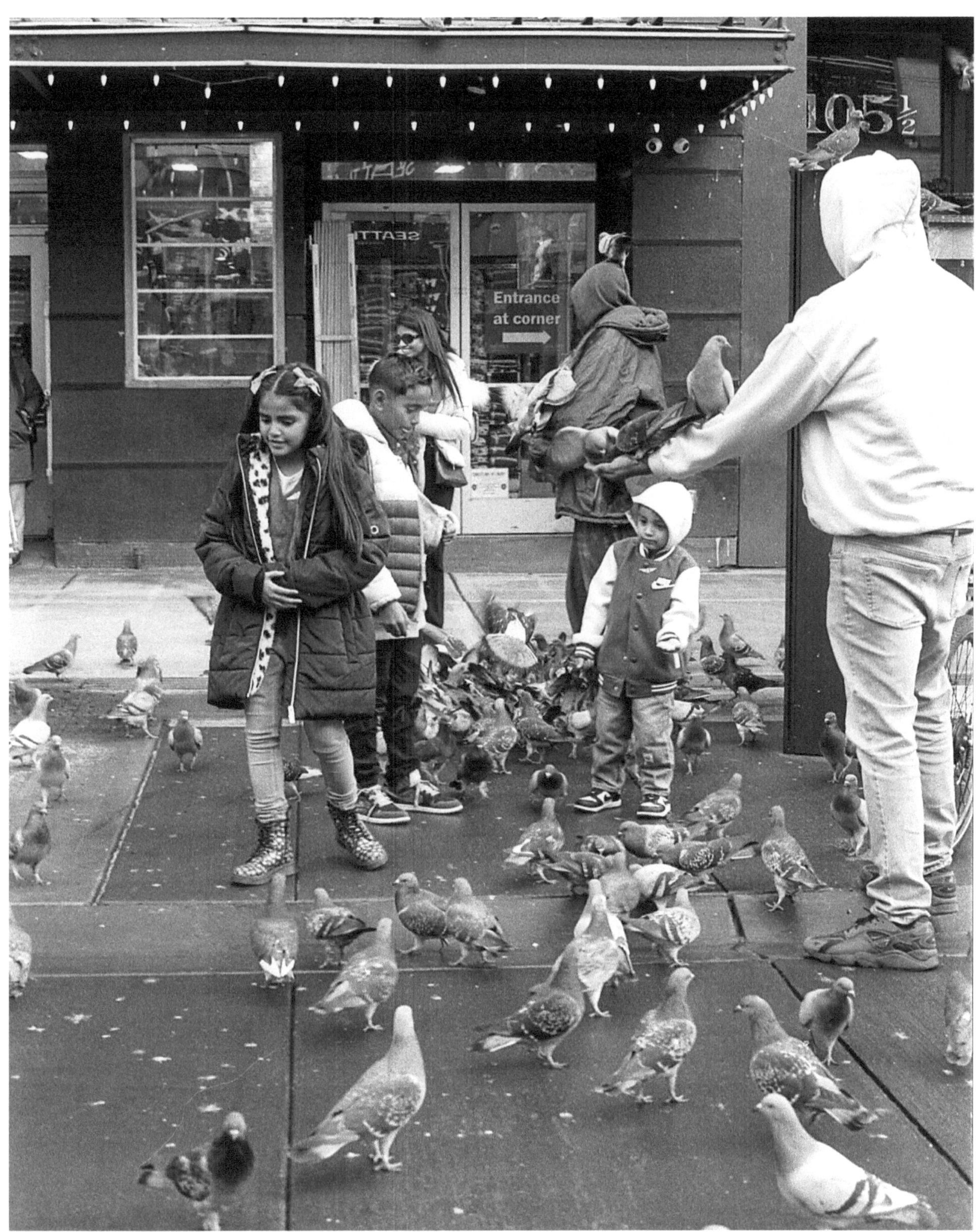

105½
Entrance
at corner
SEATTLE

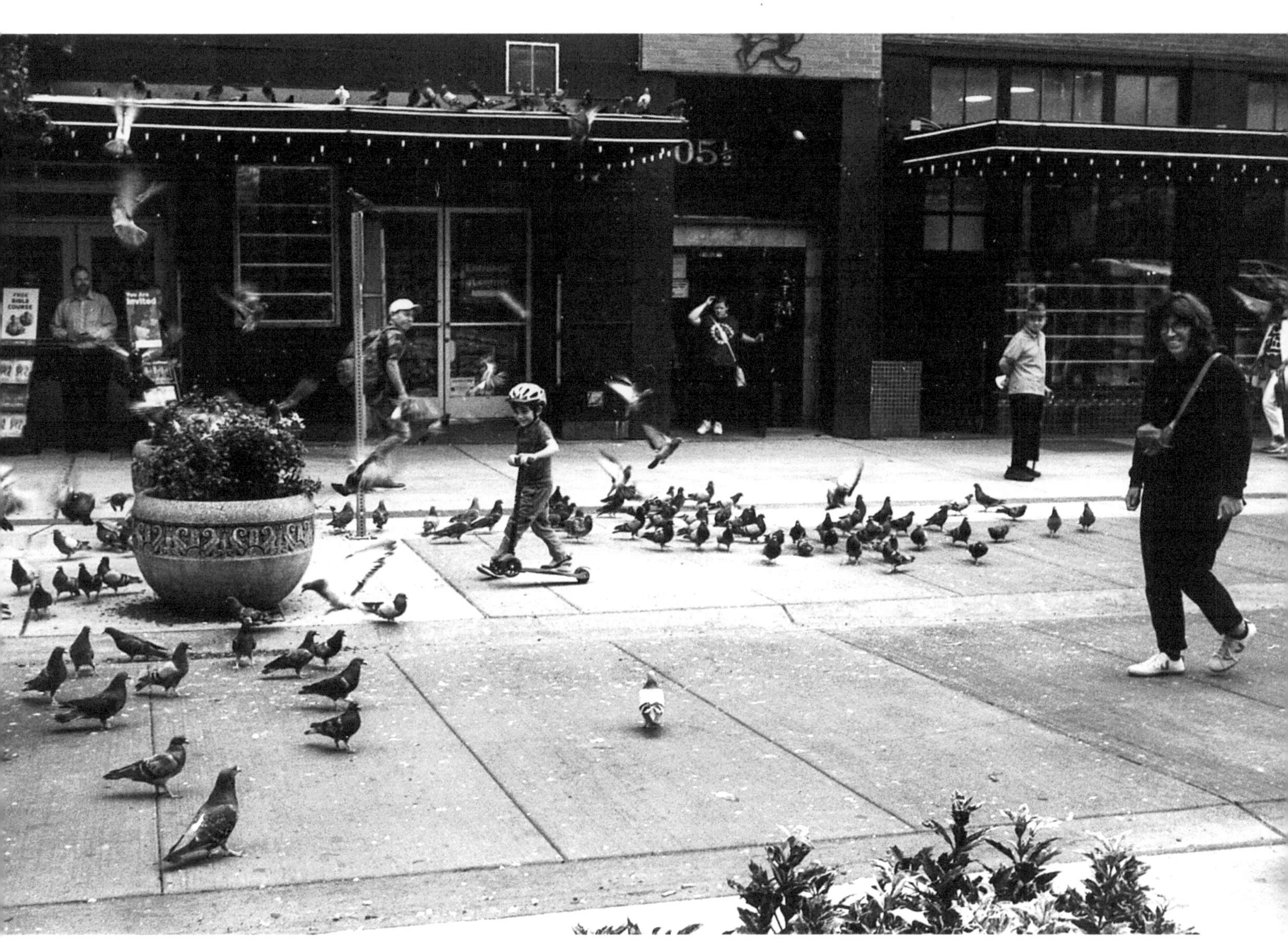

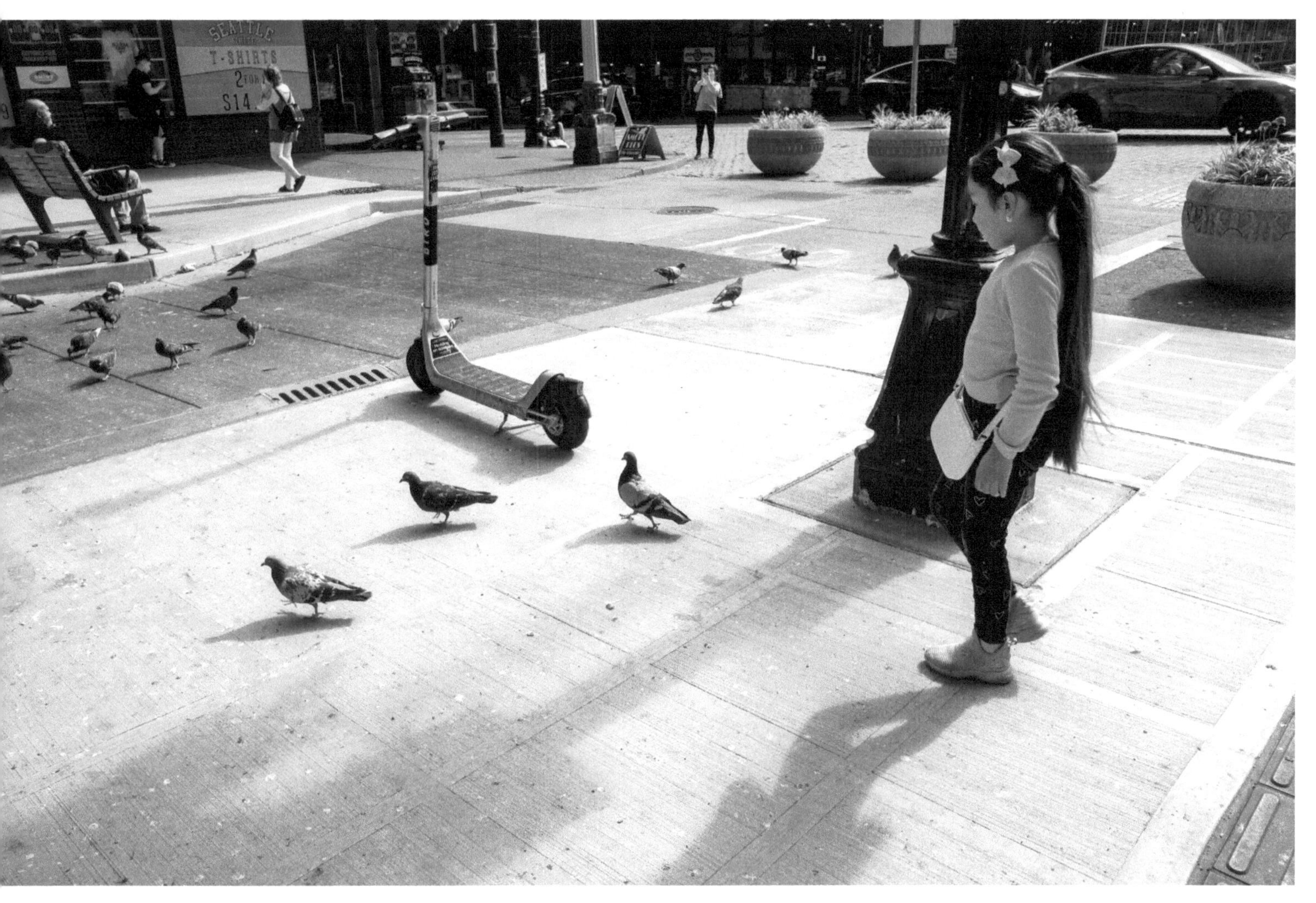
SEATTLE
T-SHIRTS
2 FOR
$14

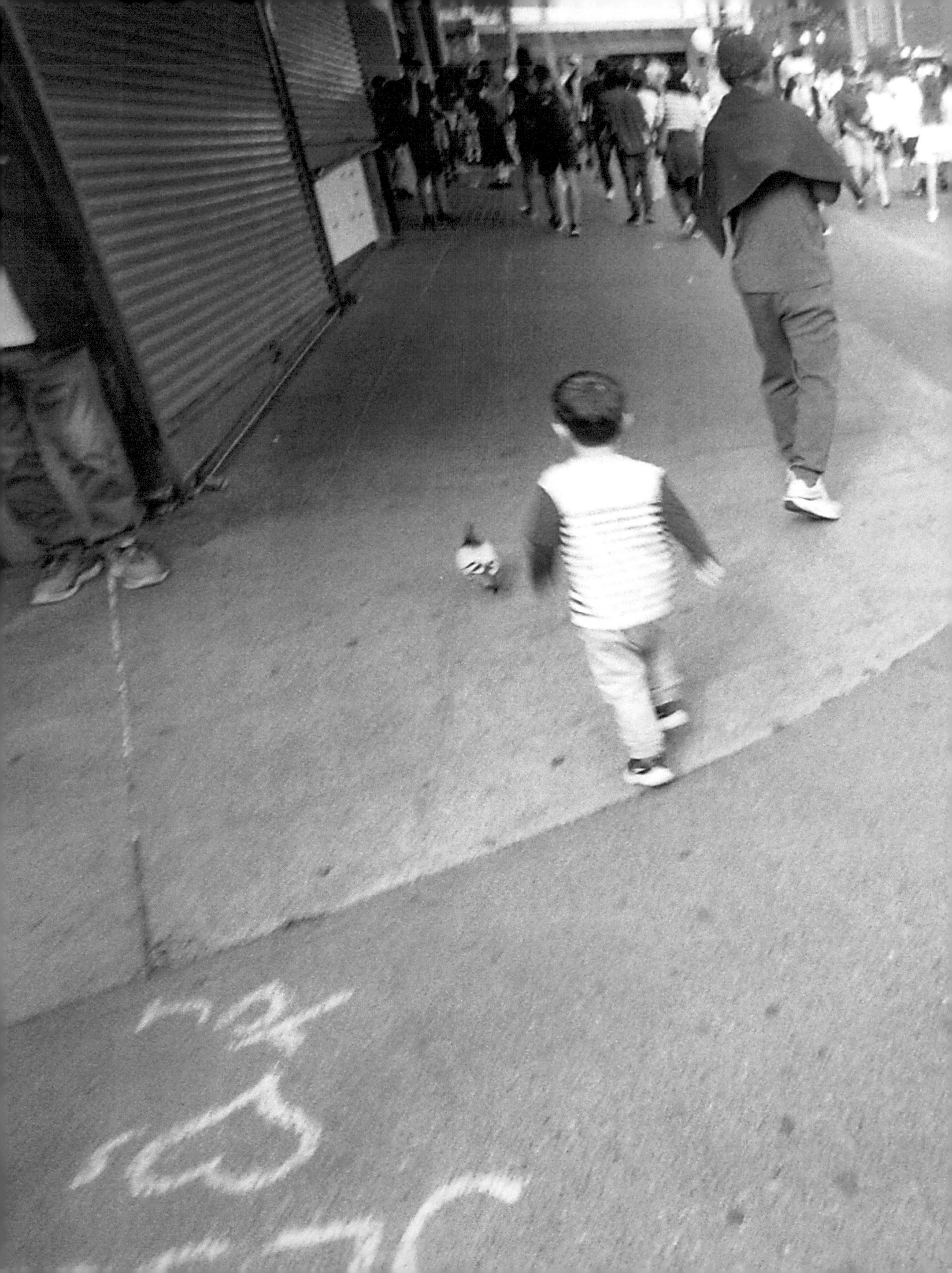

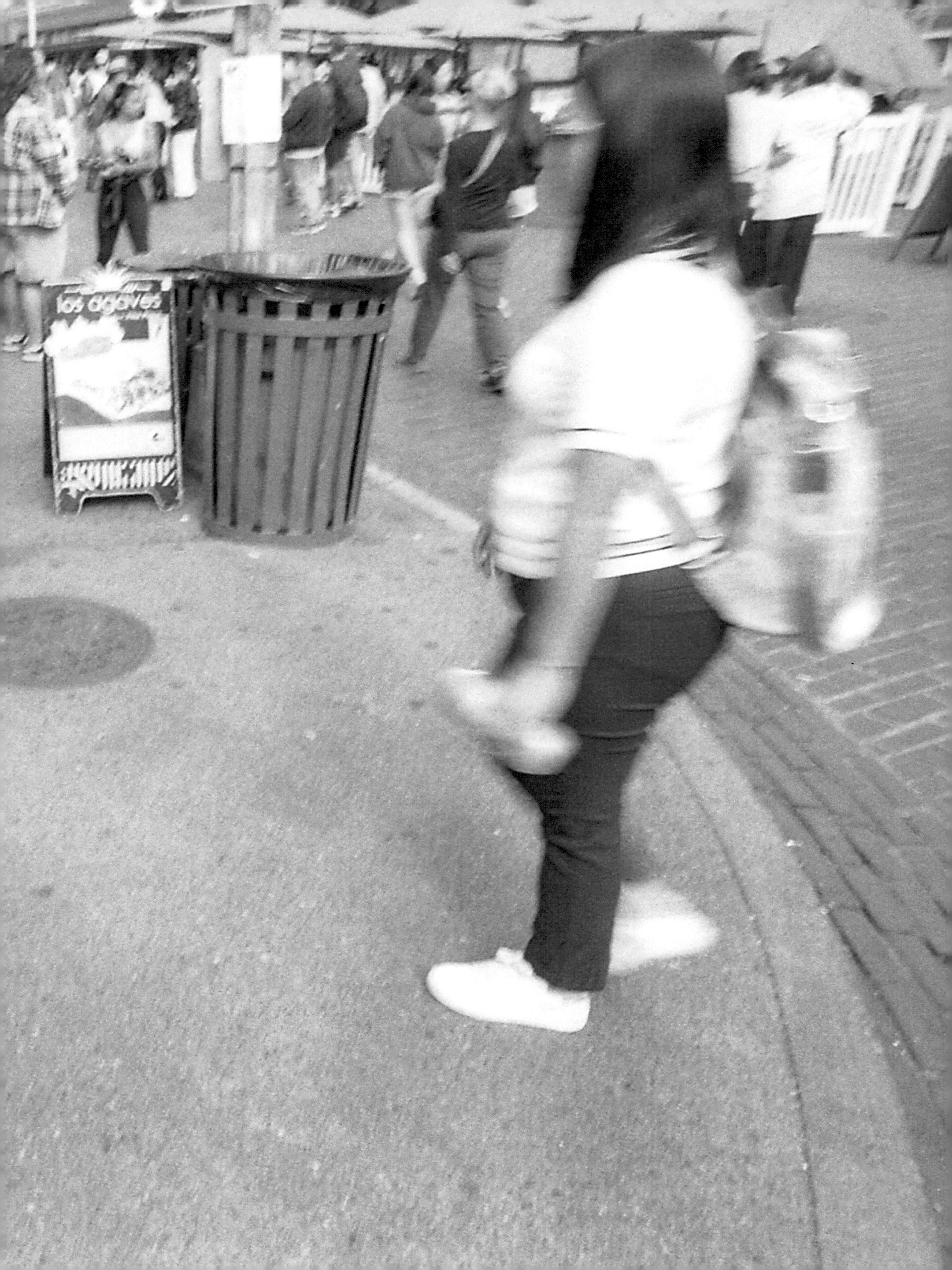
los agaves

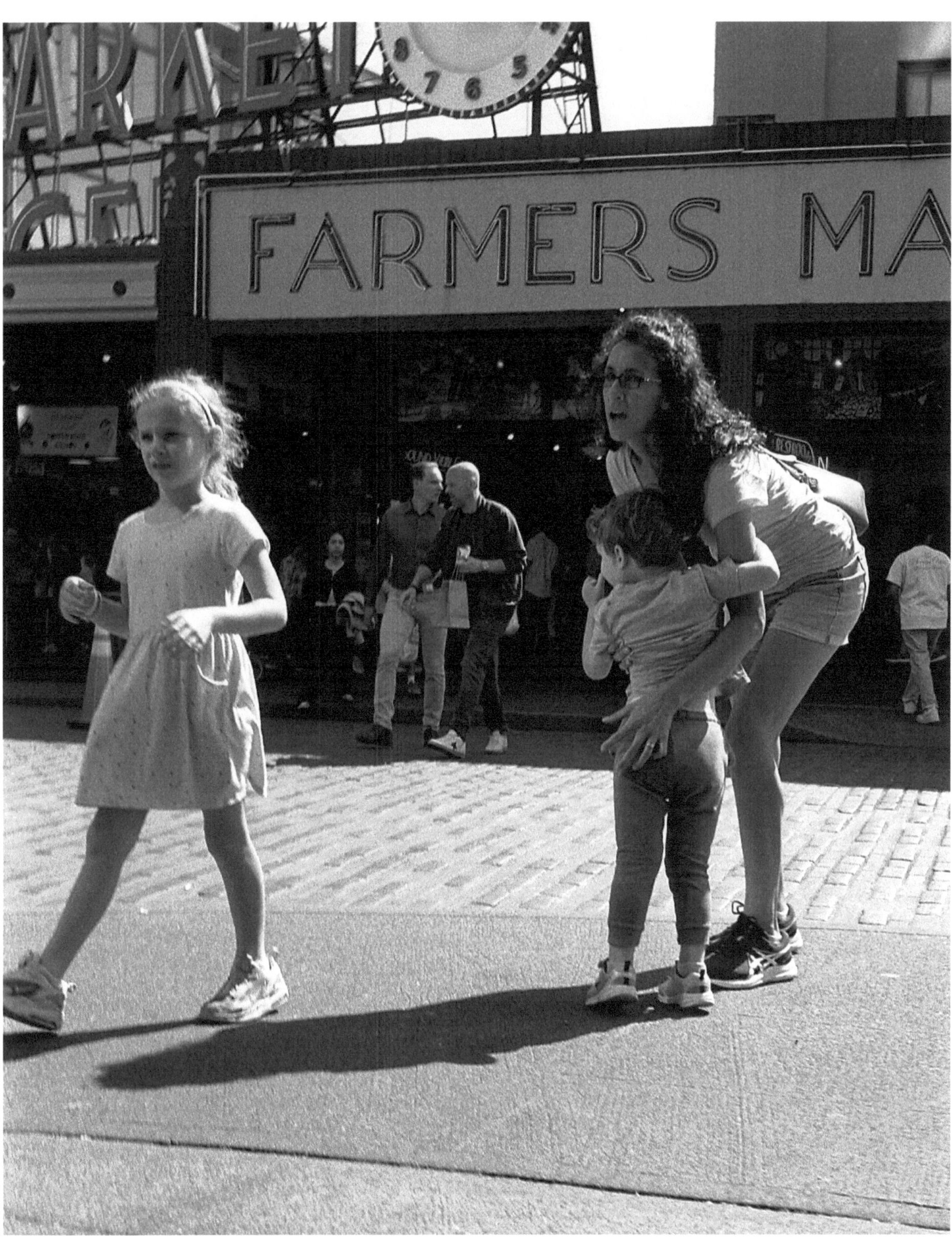
FARMERS MA

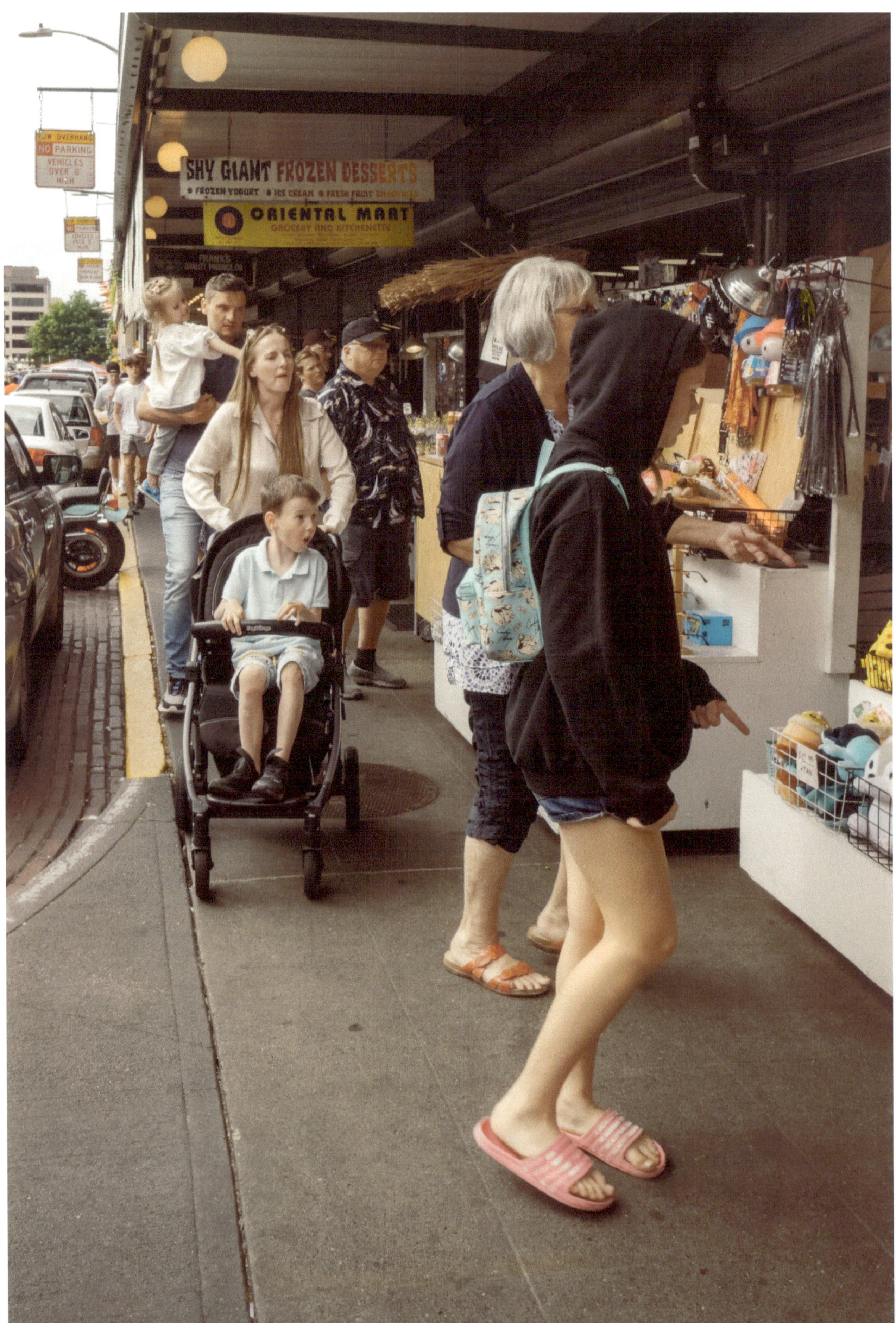
LOW OVERHANG
NO PARKING
VEHICLES
OVER 8'
HIGH
SHY GIANT FROZEN DESSERTS
FROZEN YOGURT   ICE CREAM   FRESH FRUIT SMOOTHIES
ORIENTAL MART
GROCERY AND KITCHENETTE
FRANK'S

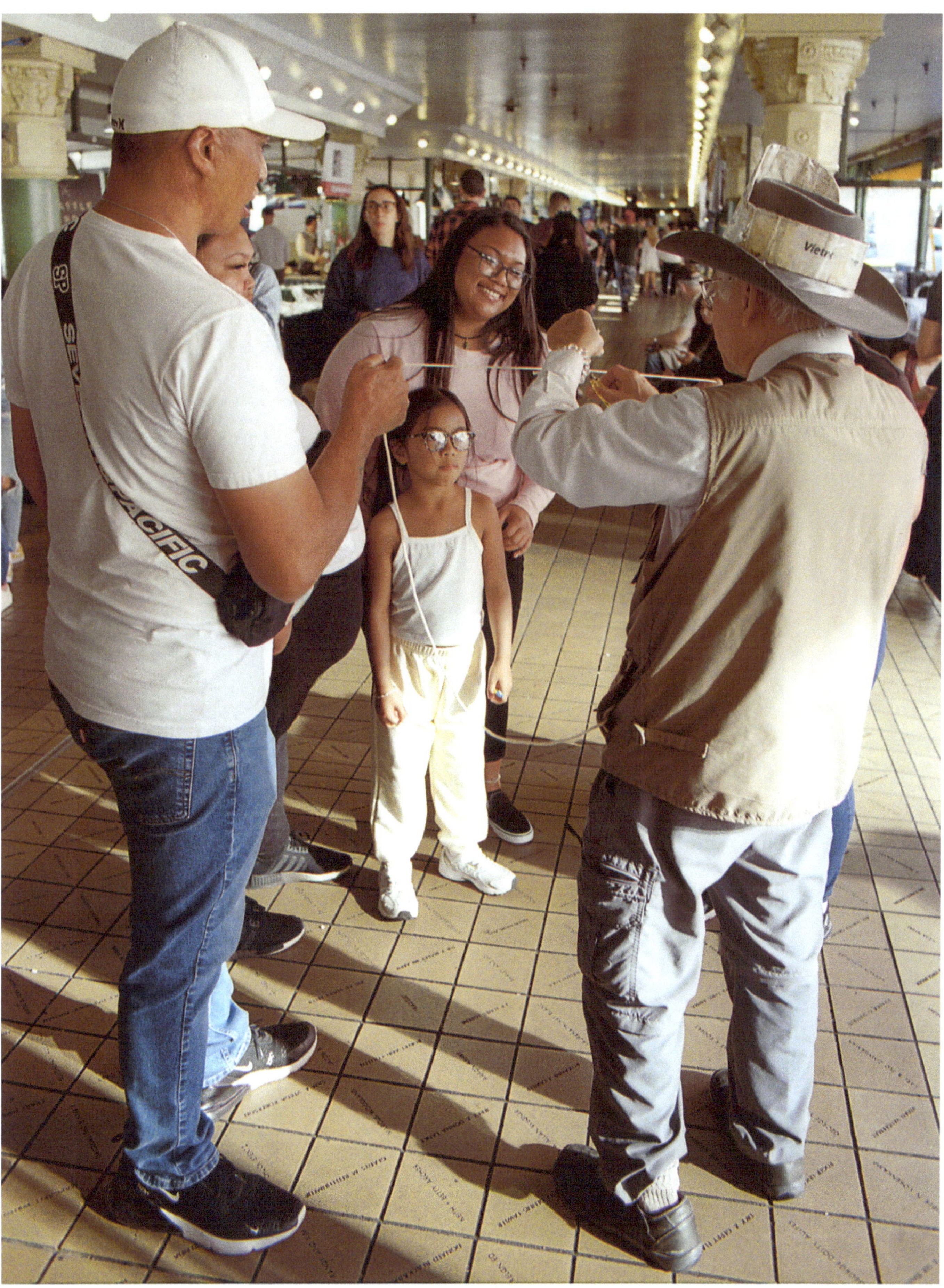

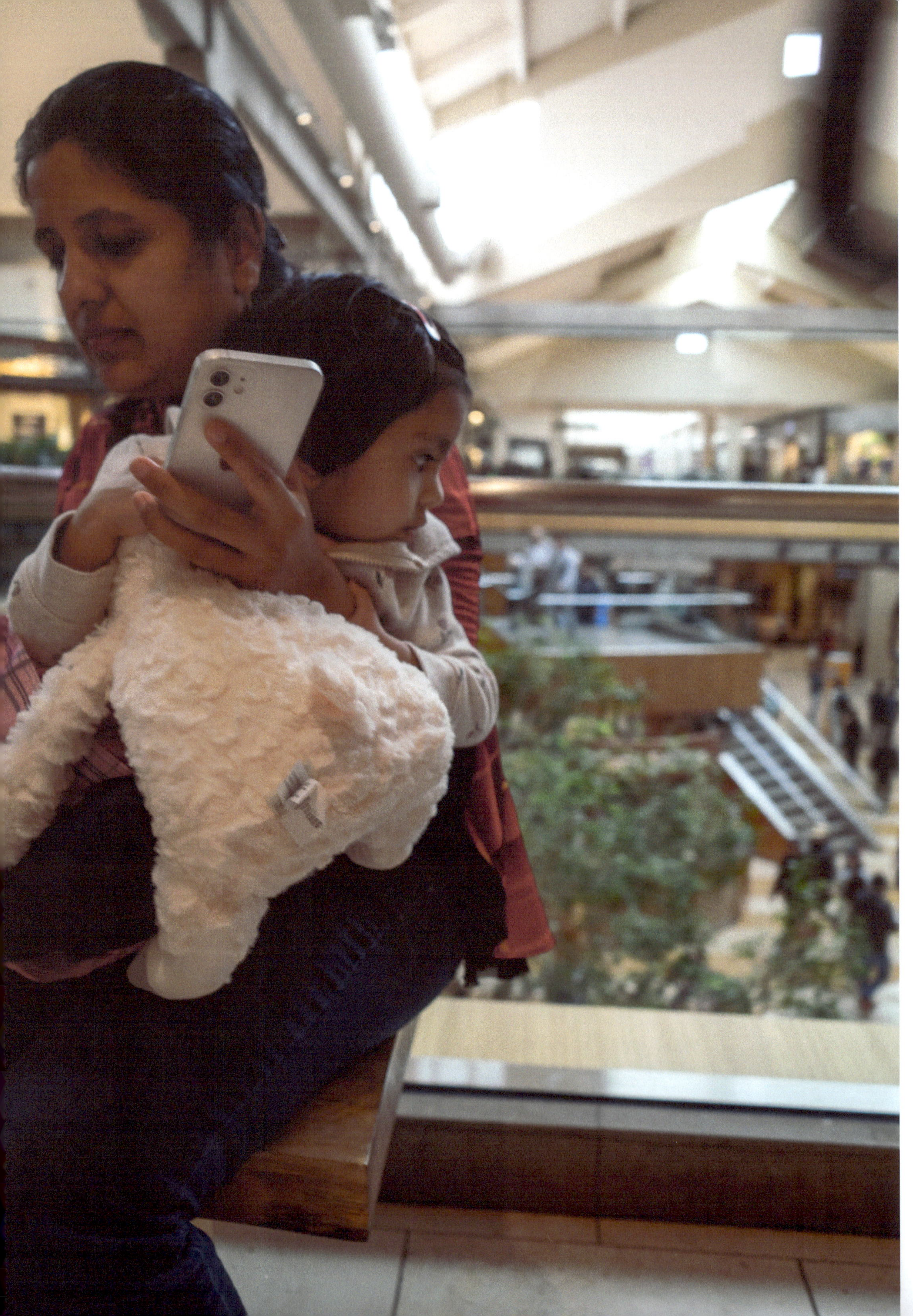

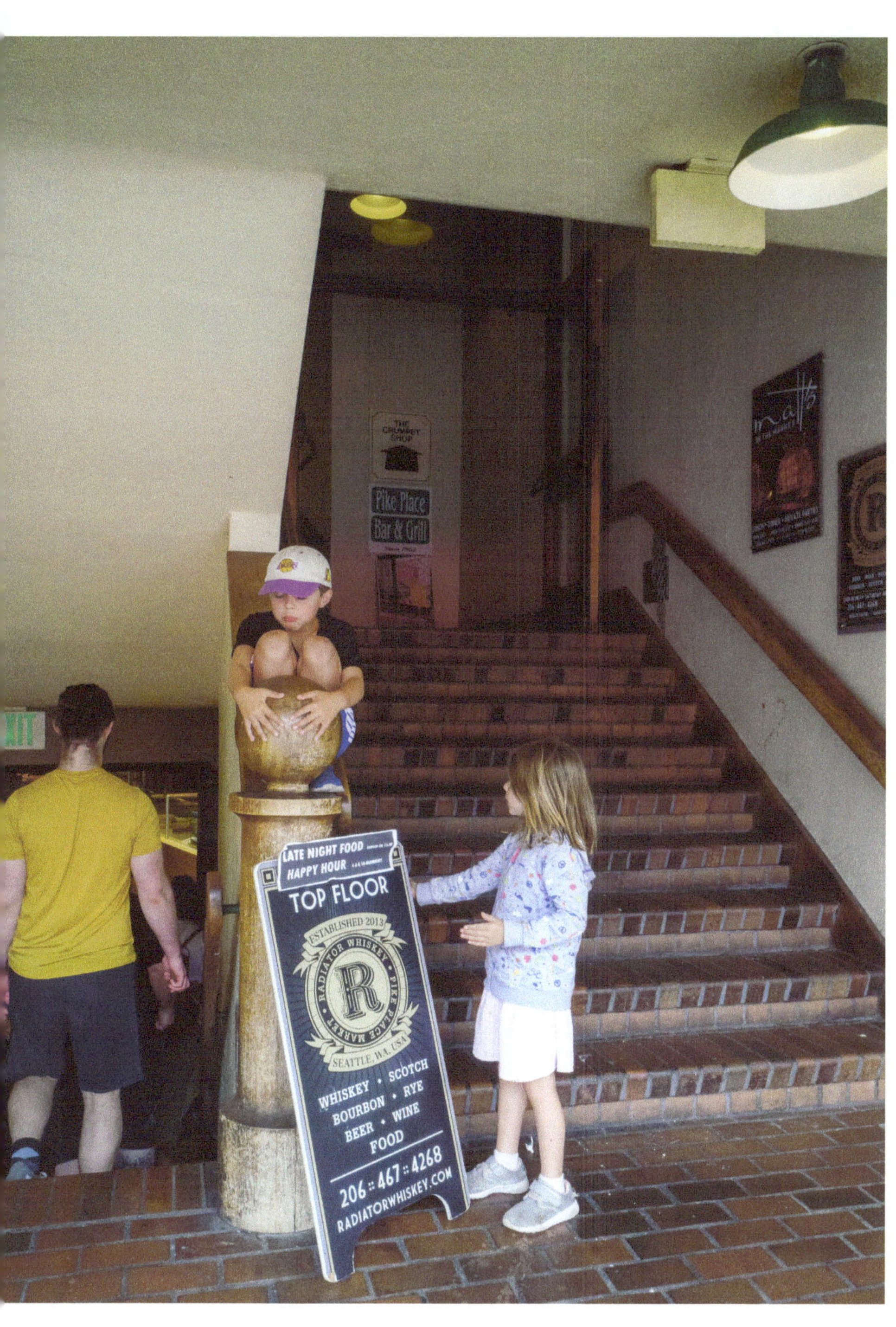
THE CRUMPET SHOP
Pike Place
Bar & Grill
matt's
LATE NIGHT FOOD
HAPPY HOUR
TOP FLOOR
ESTABLISHED 2013
RADIATOR WHISKEY
PIKE PLACE MARKET
R
SEATTLE WA, USA
WHISKEY • SCOTCH
BOURBON • RYE
BEER • WINE
FOOD
206 :: 467 :: 4268
RADIATORWHISKEY.COM
EXIT

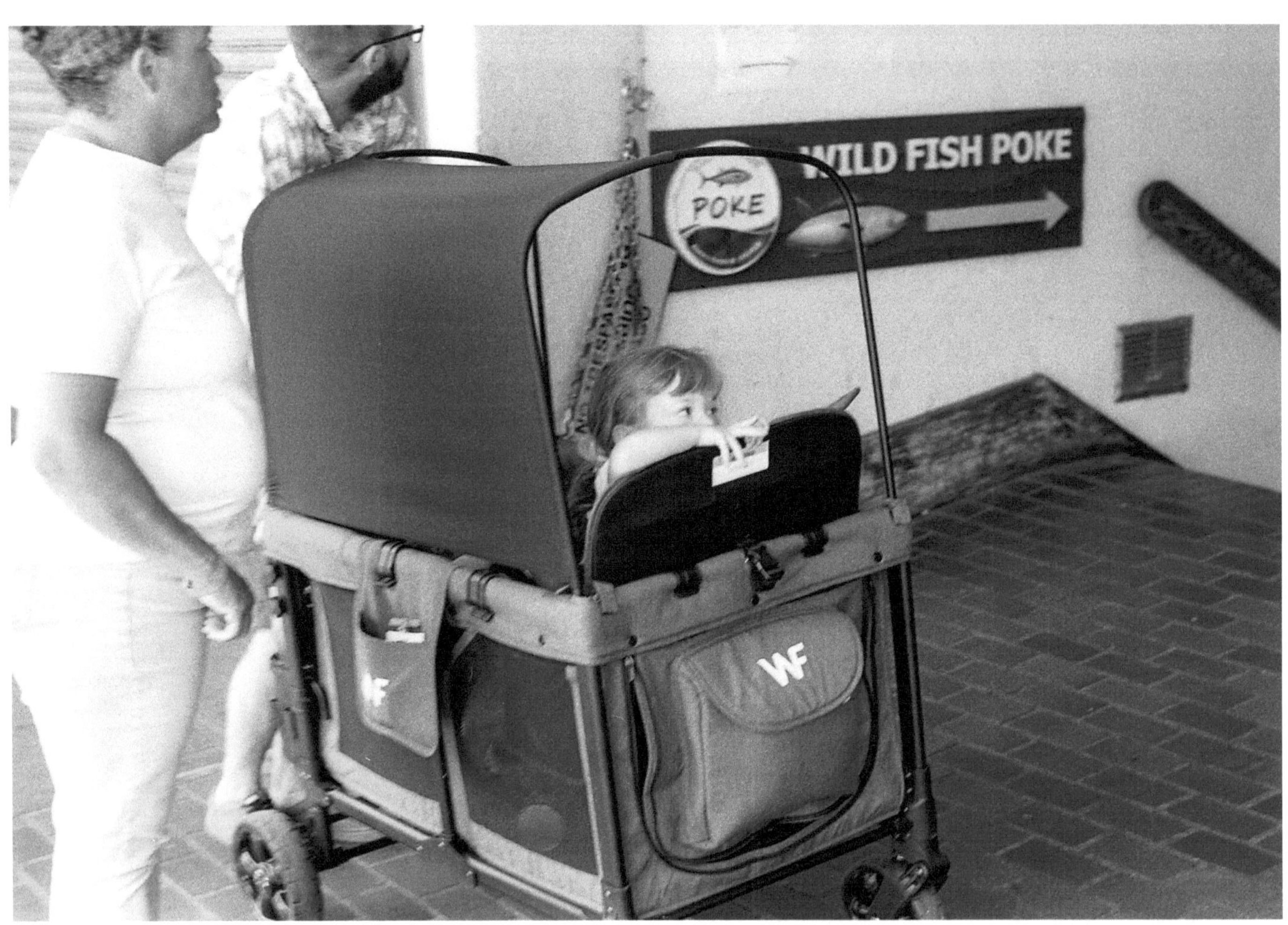
POKE
WILD FISH POKE

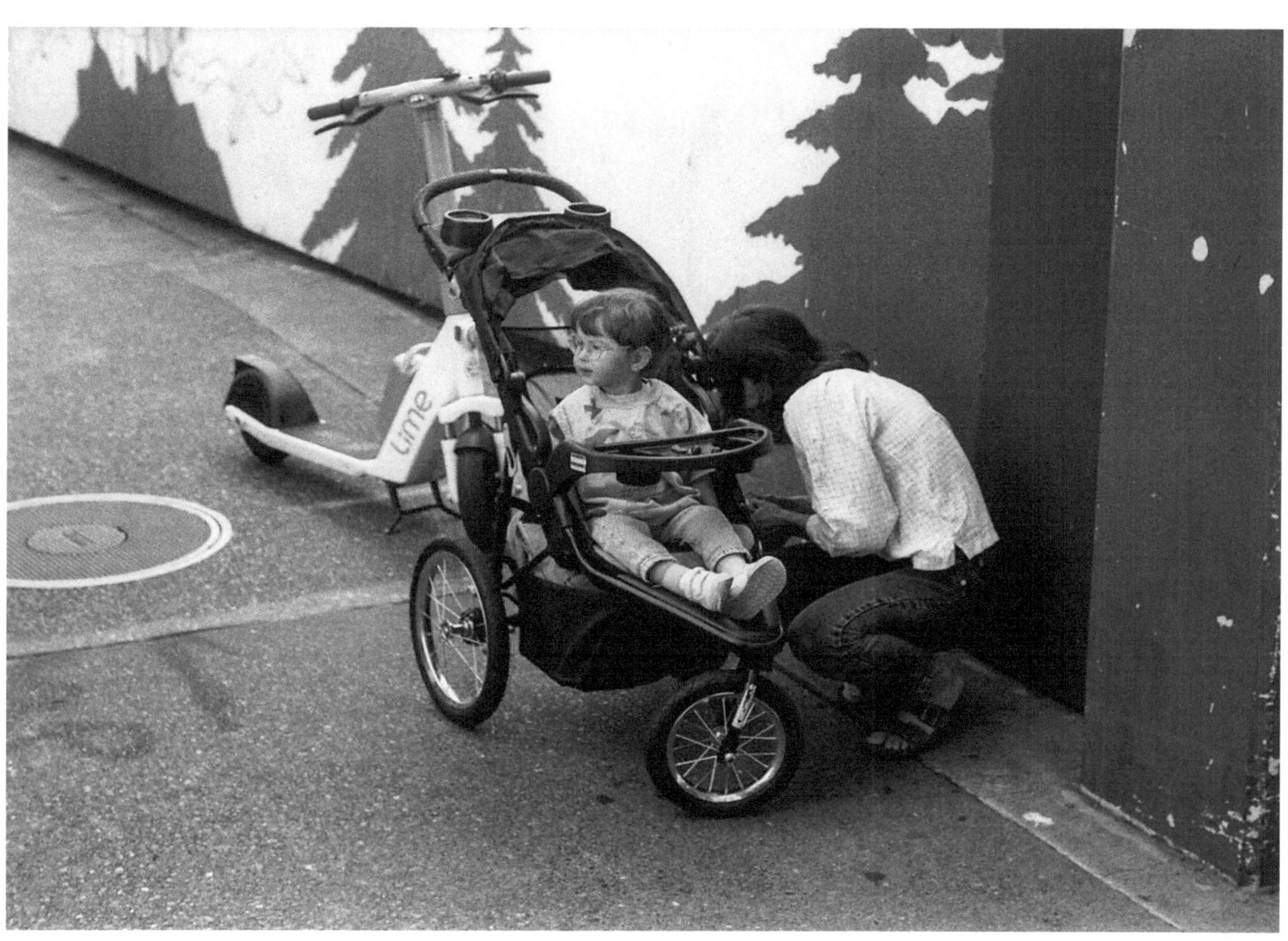

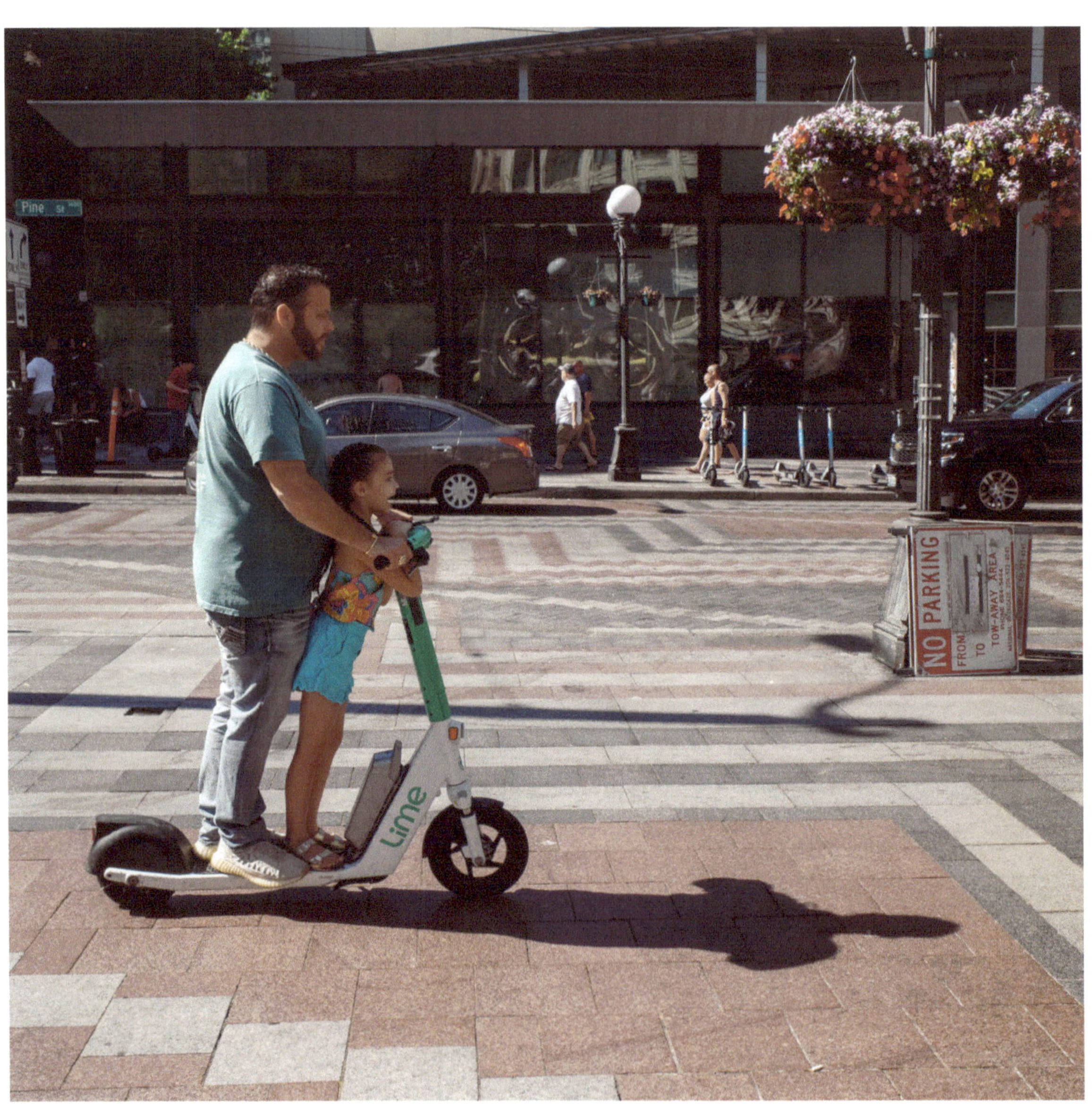

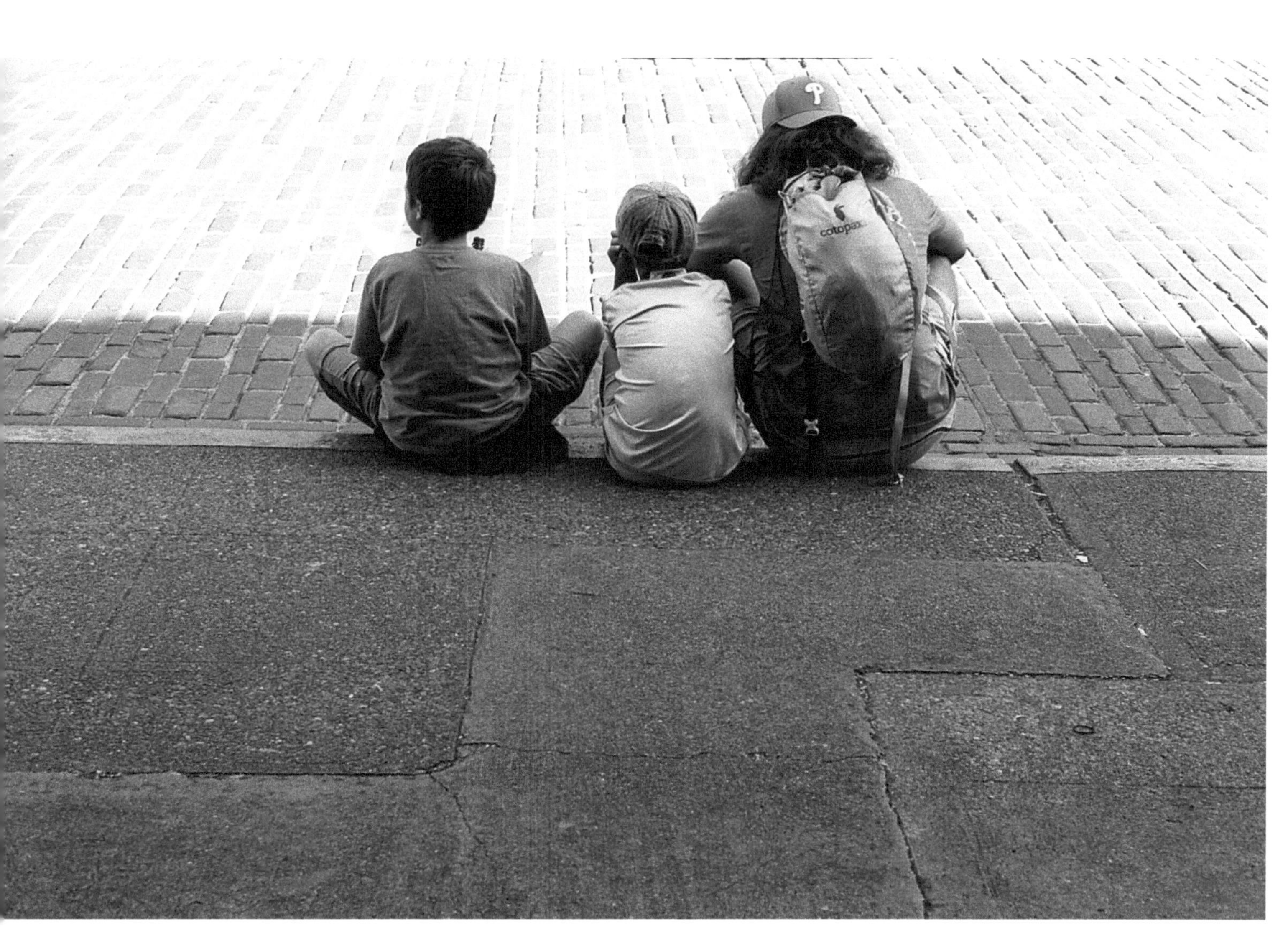

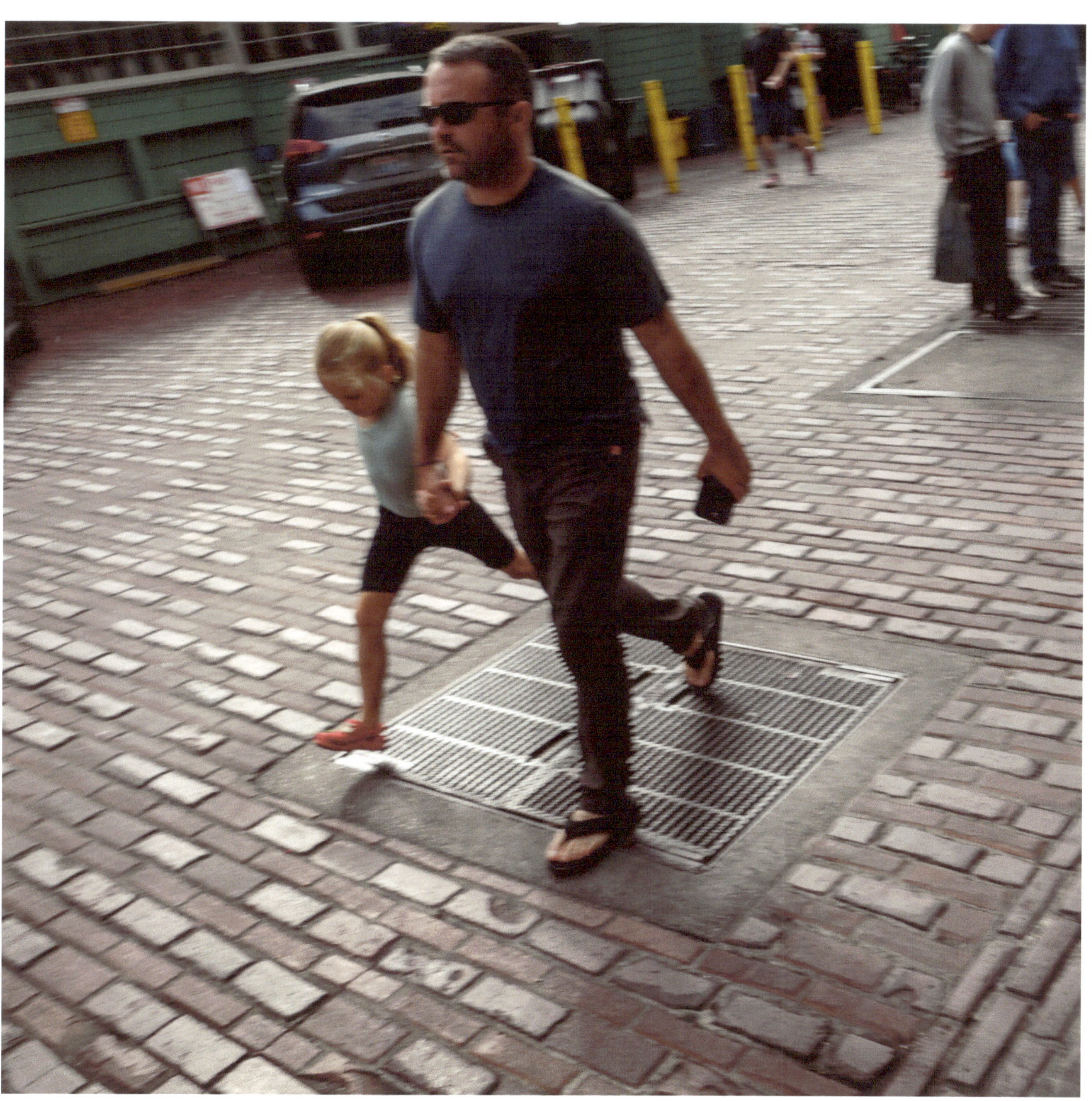

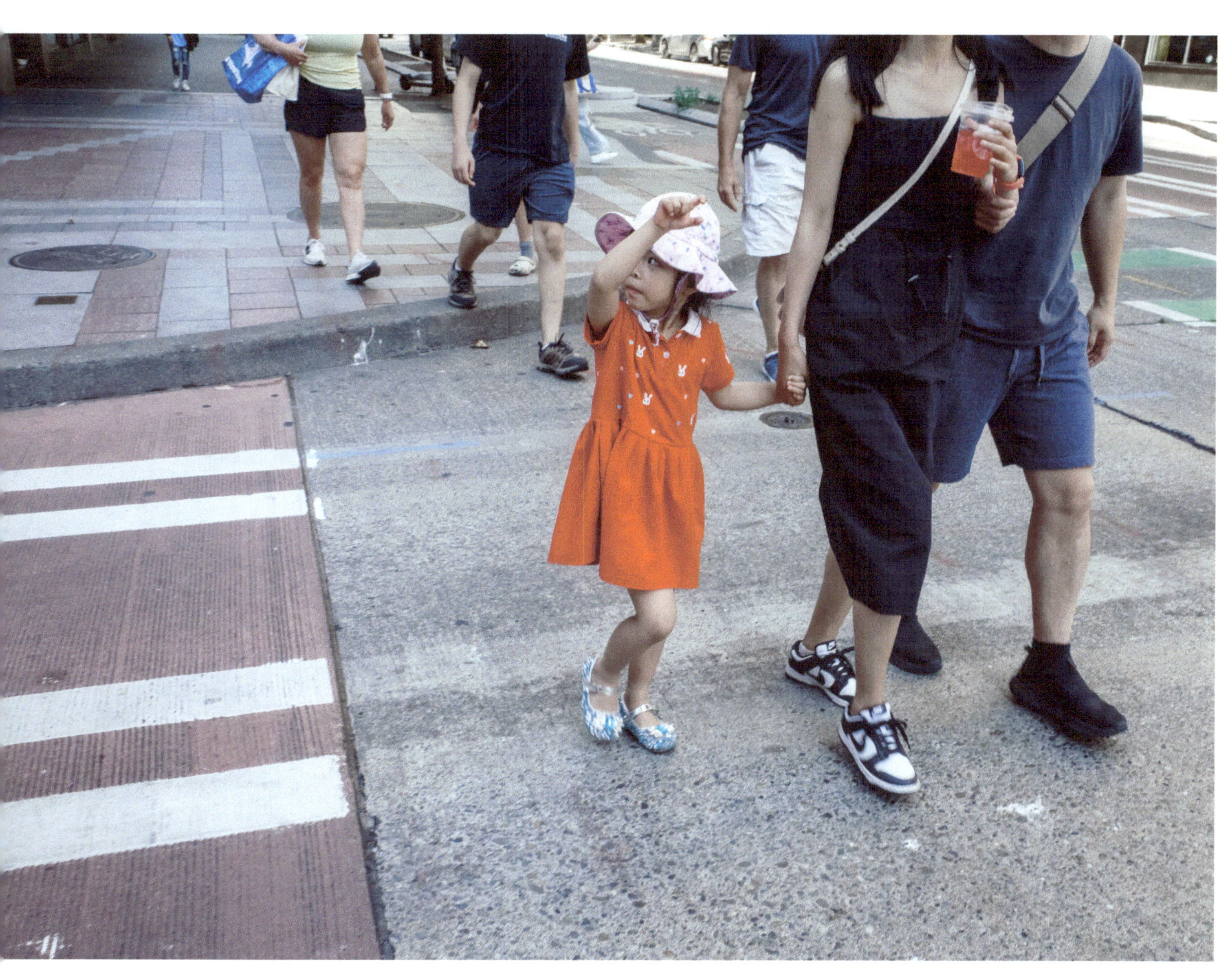

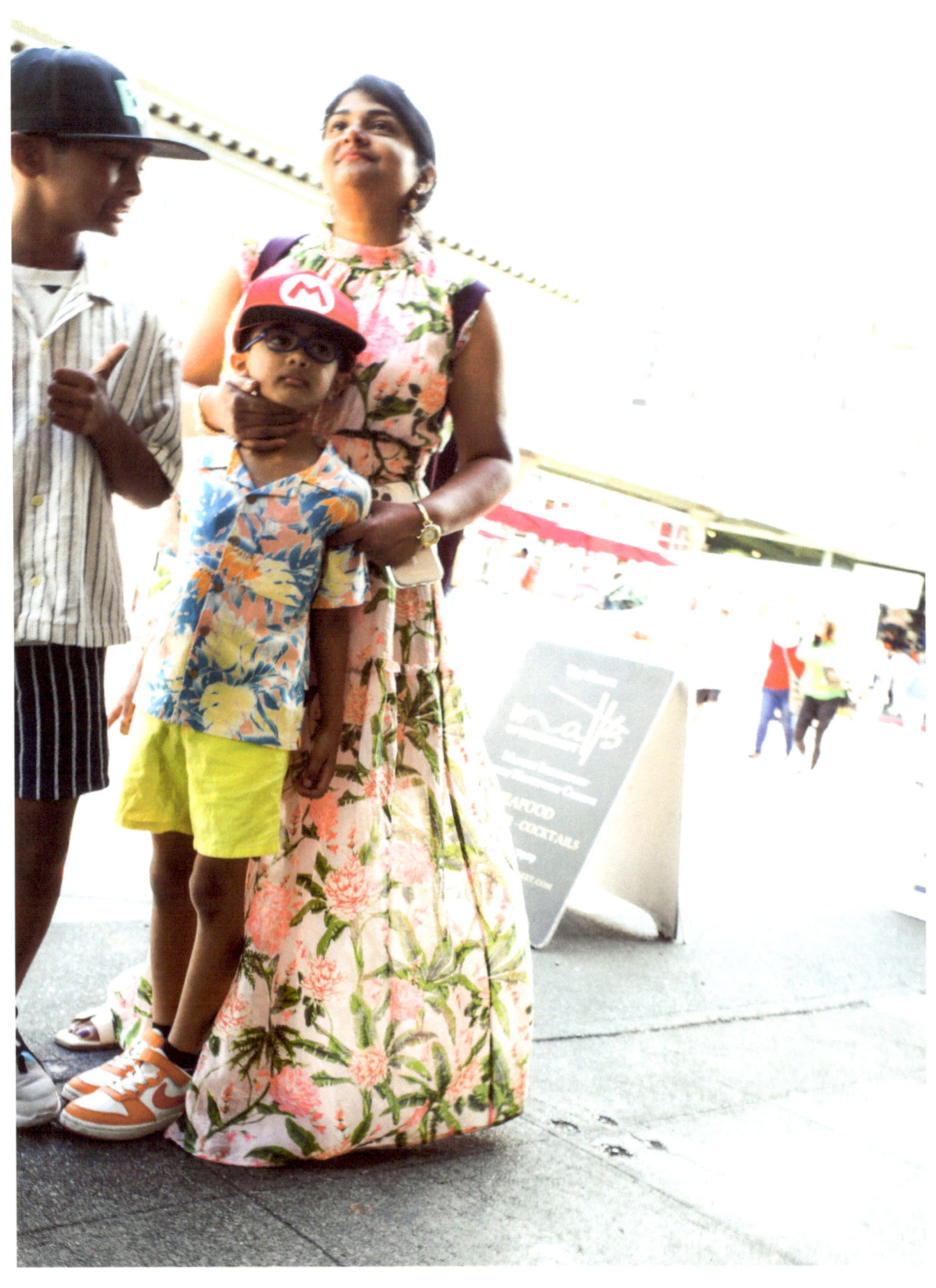
SEAFOOD
COCKTAILS

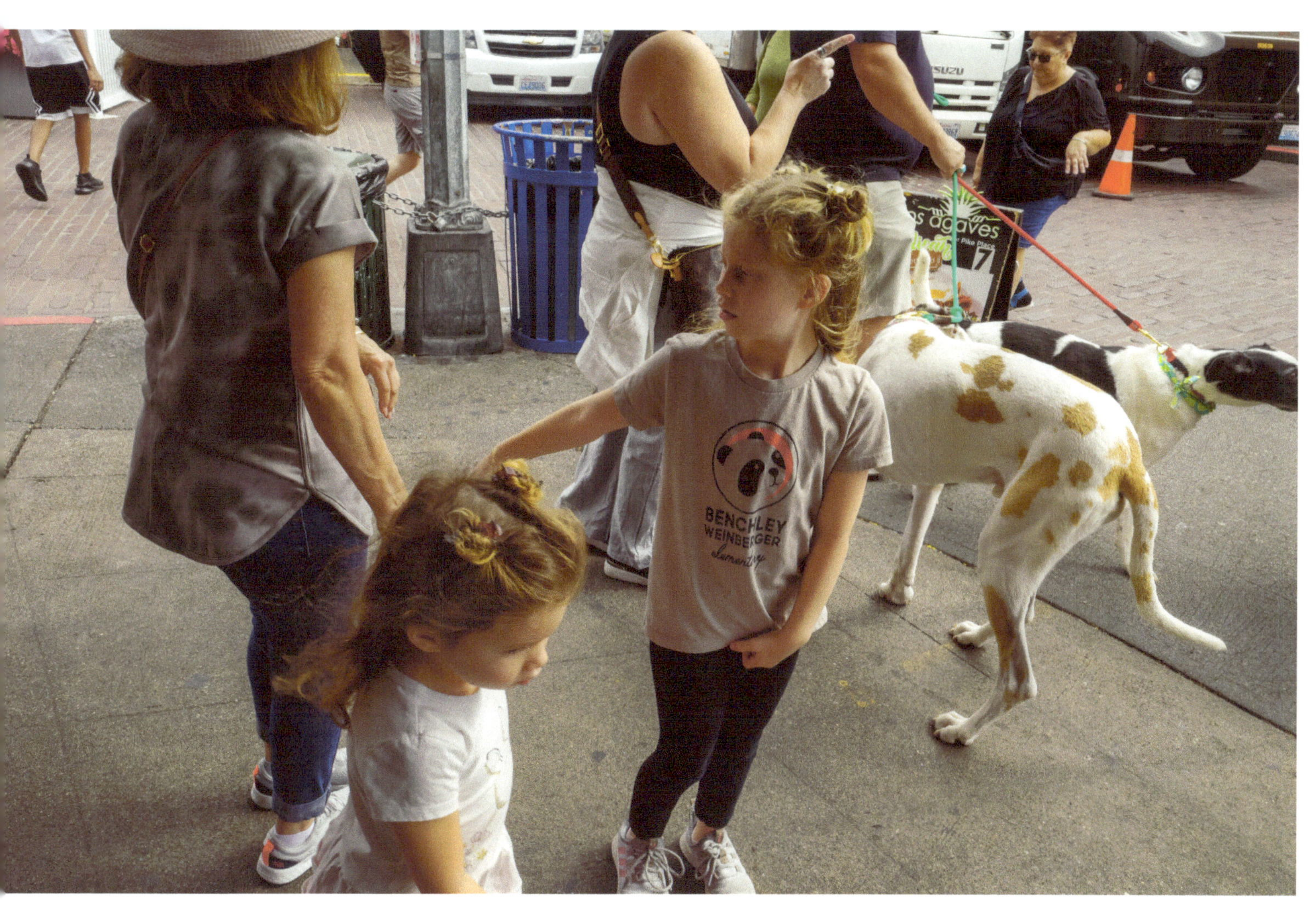
BENCHLEY
WEINBERGER
elementary
os agaves
17

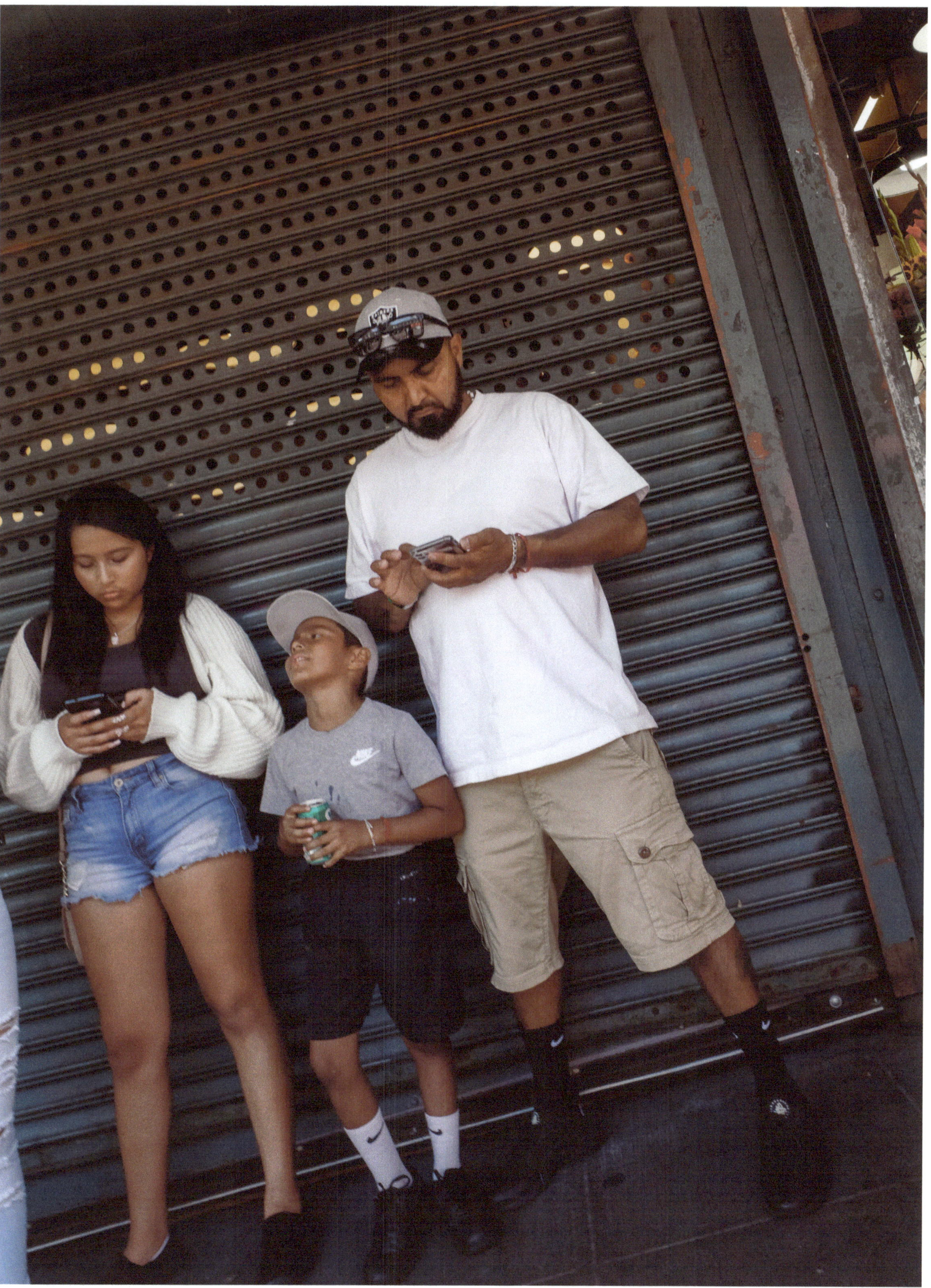

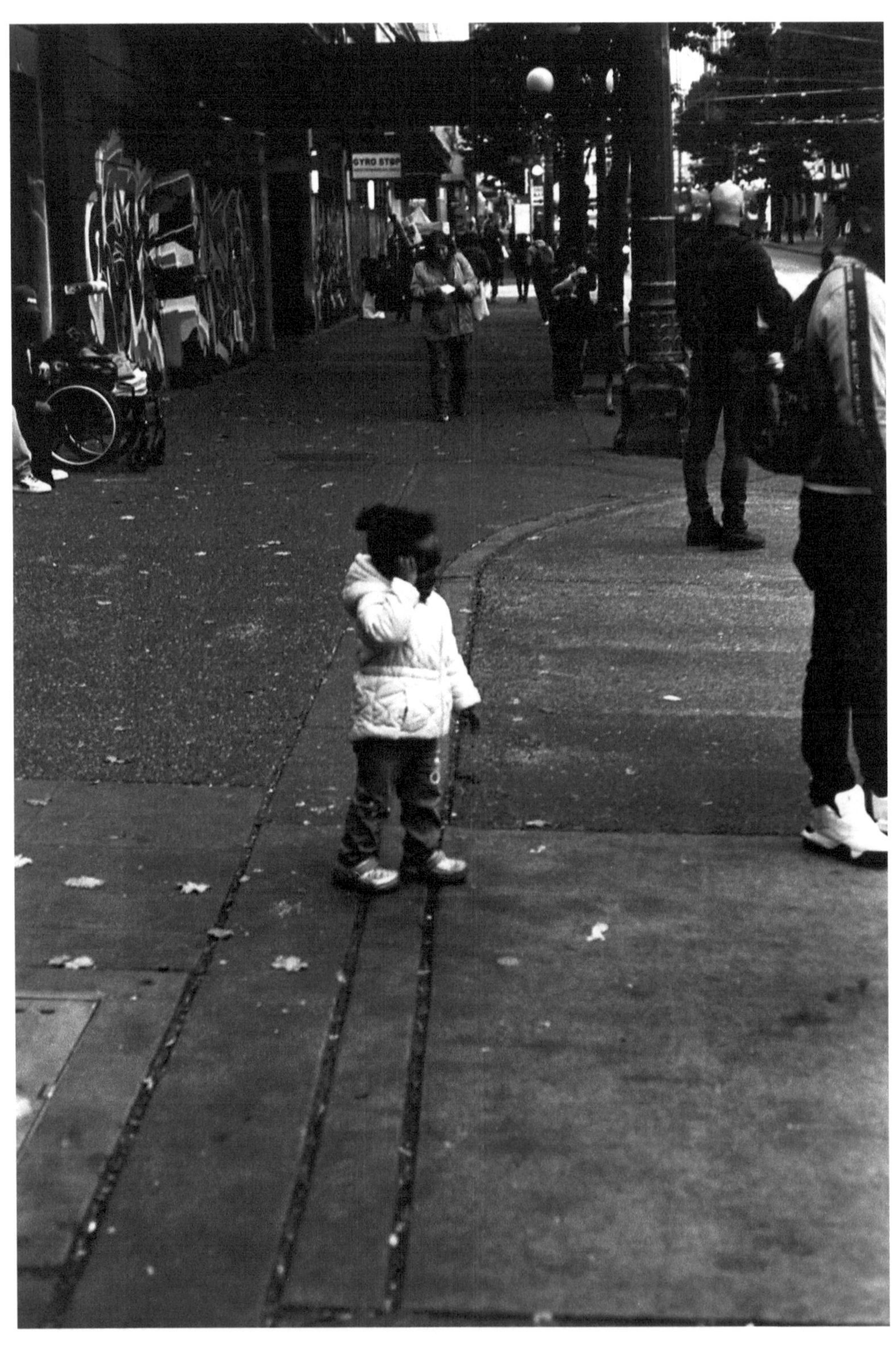

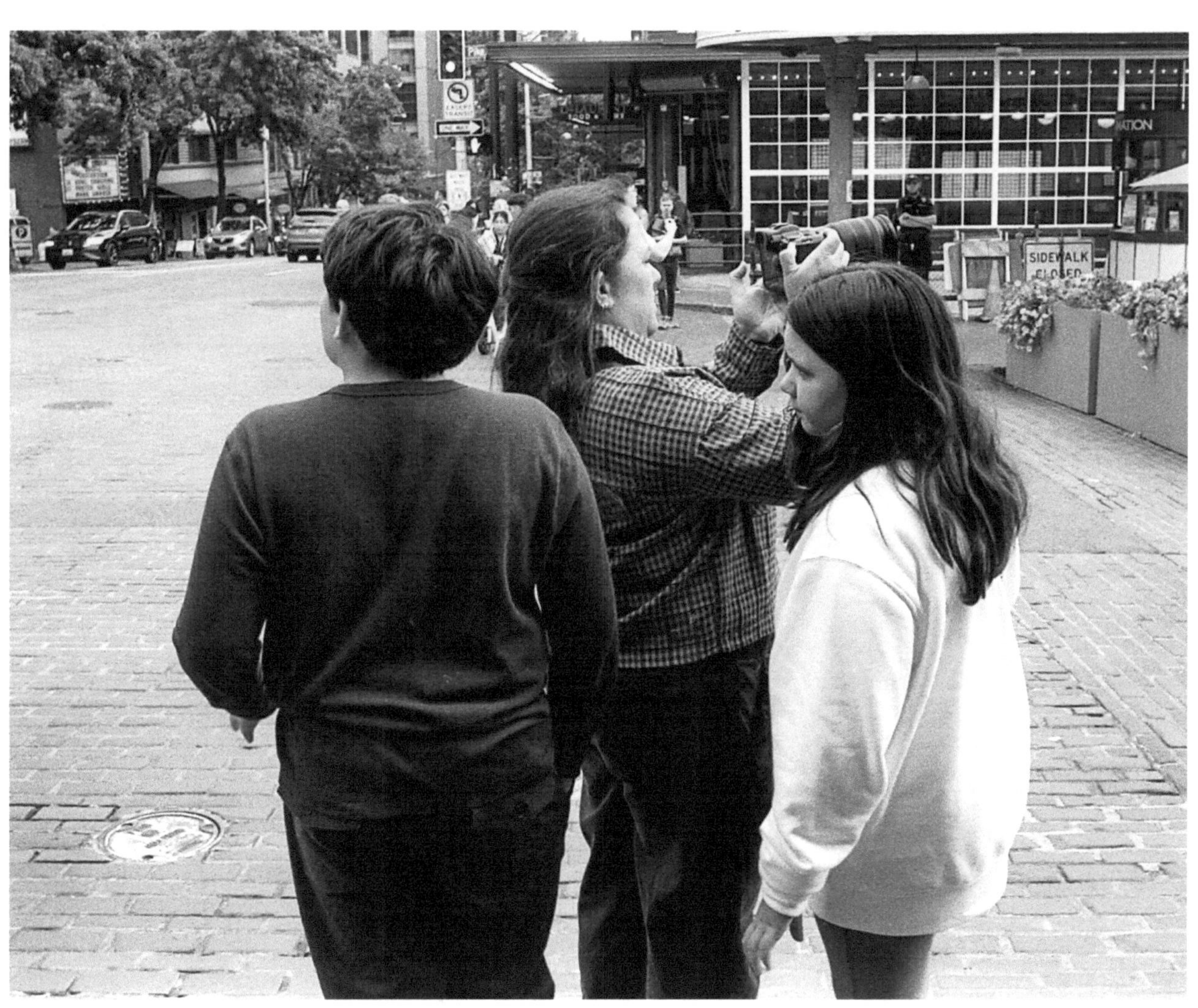

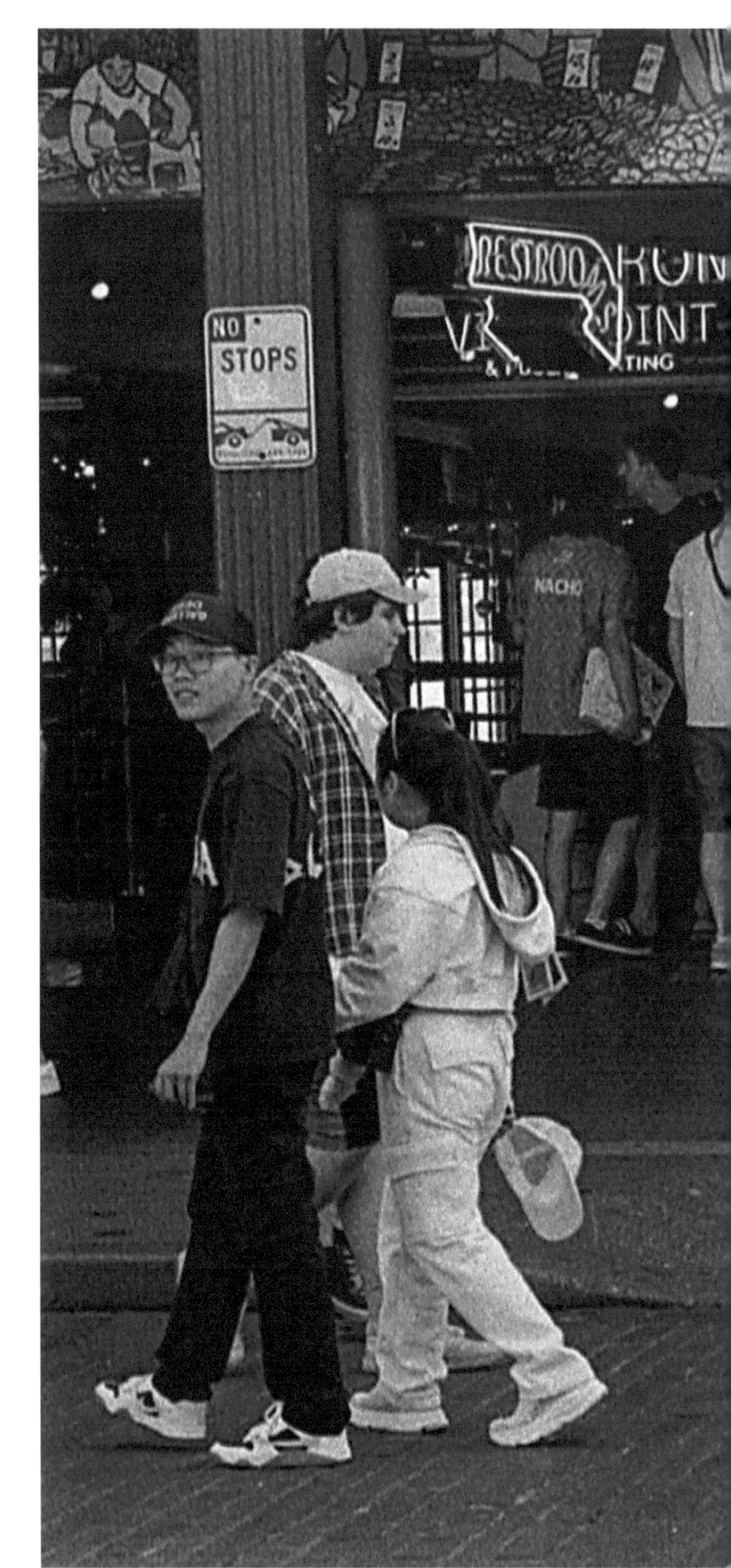

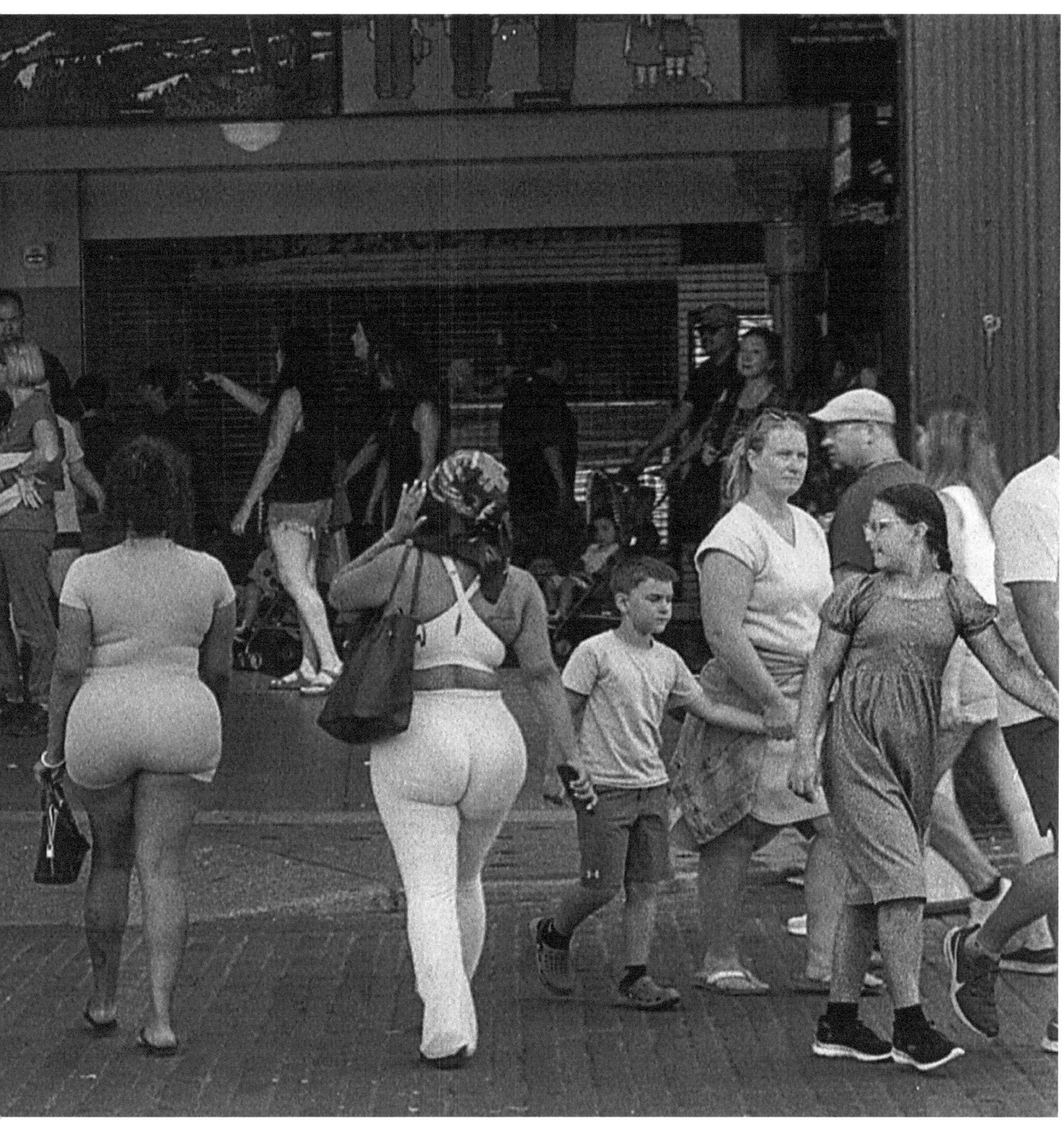

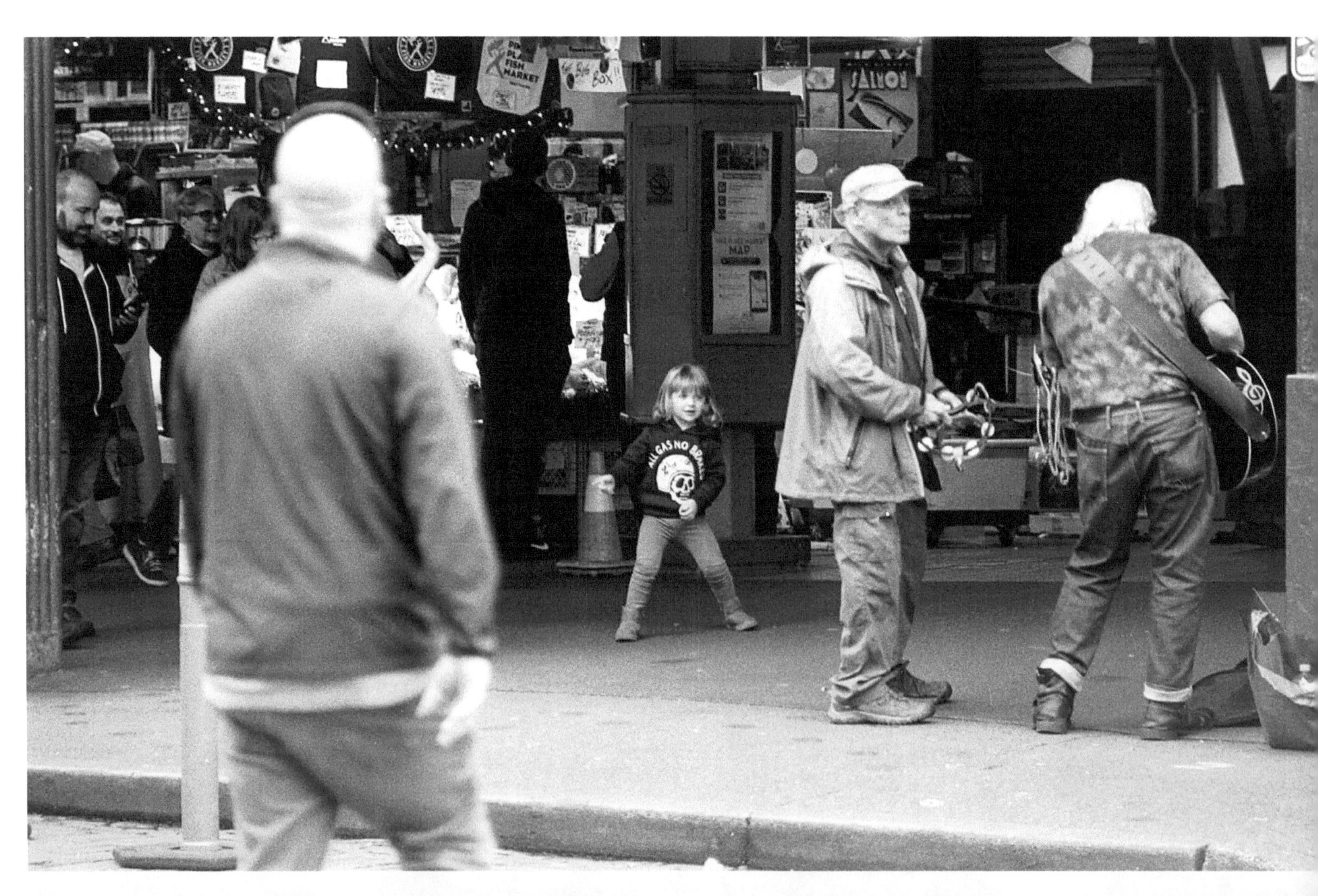
PIKE
PLACE
FISH
MARKET
SALMON
ALL GAS NO BRAKES

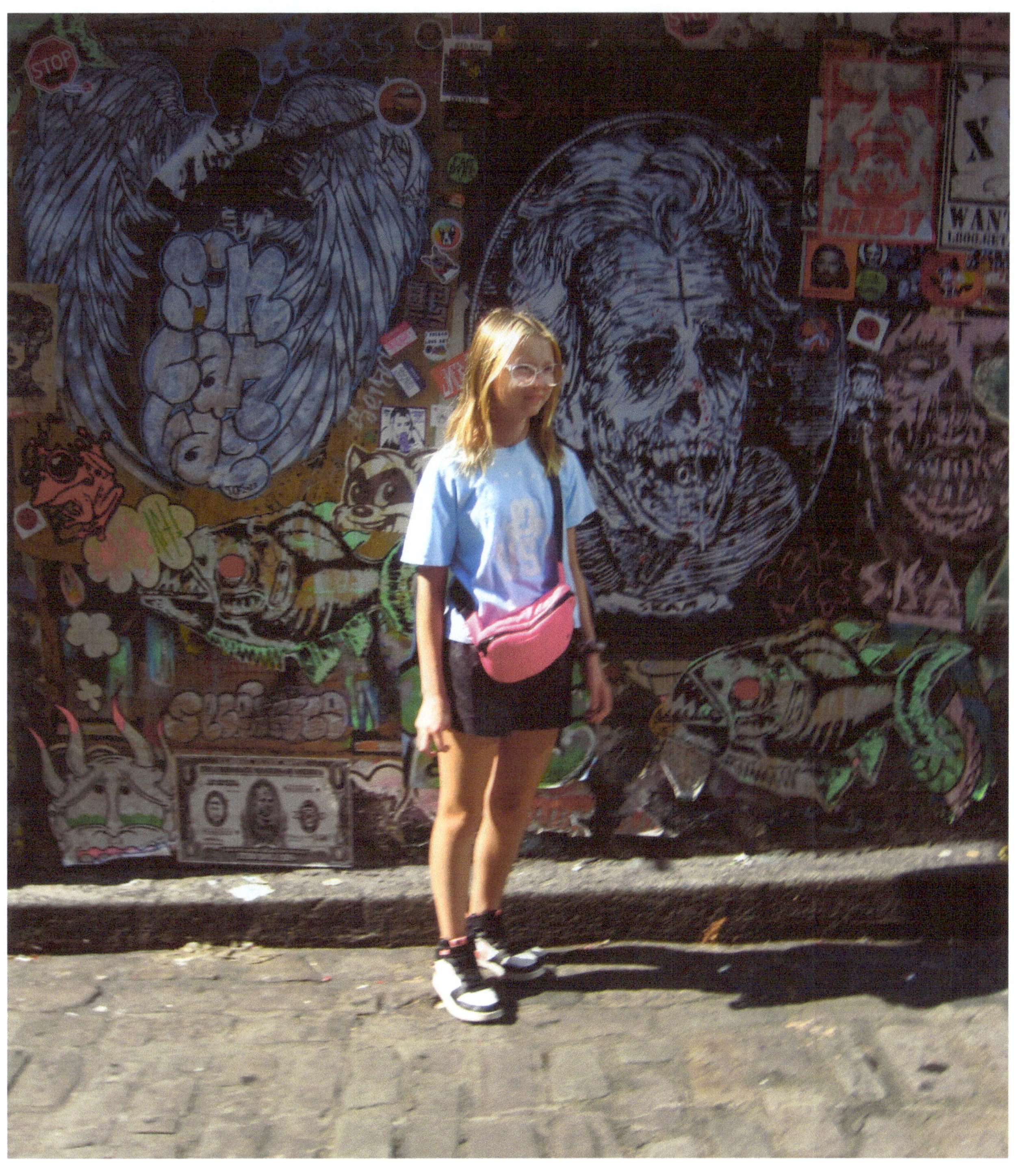

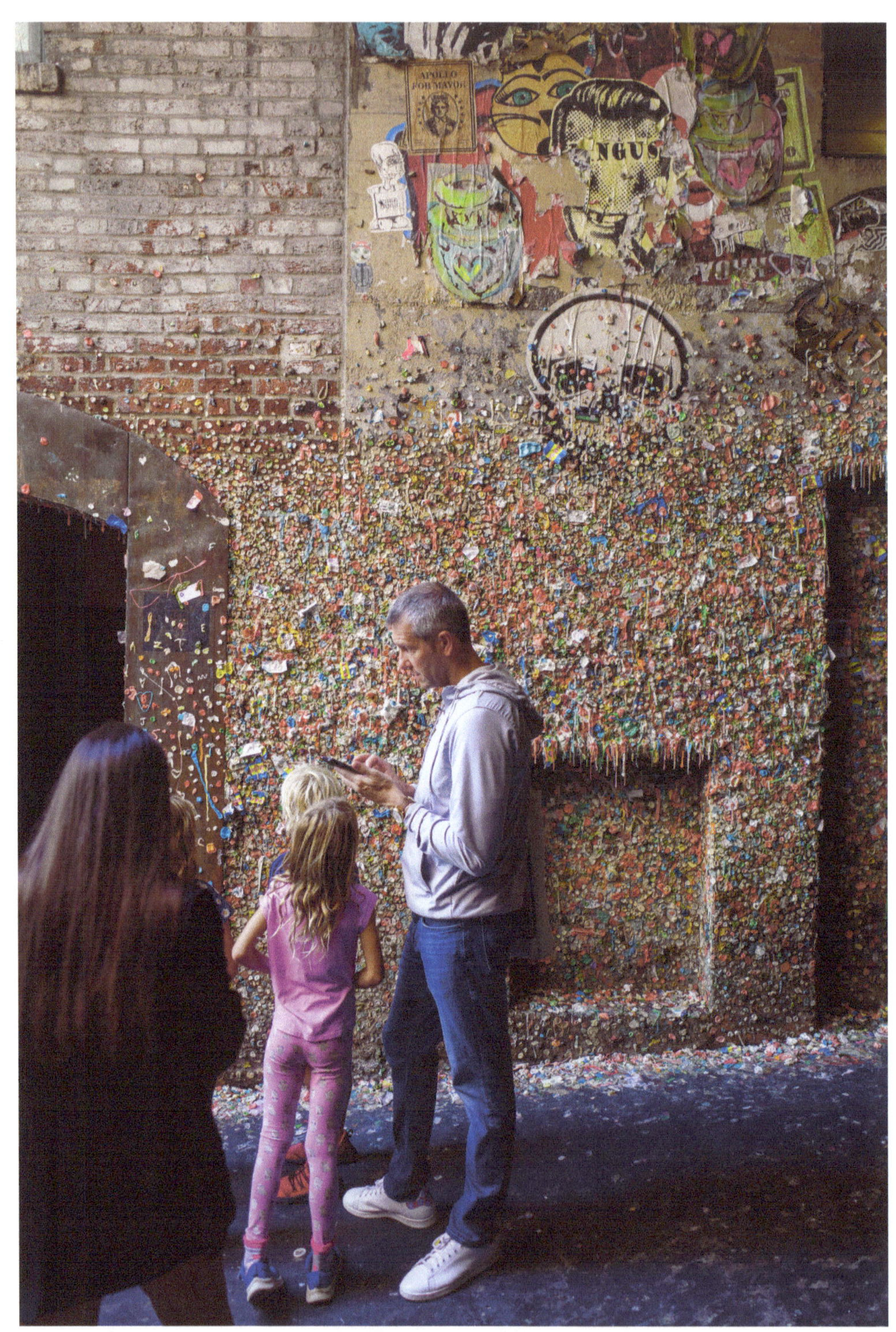

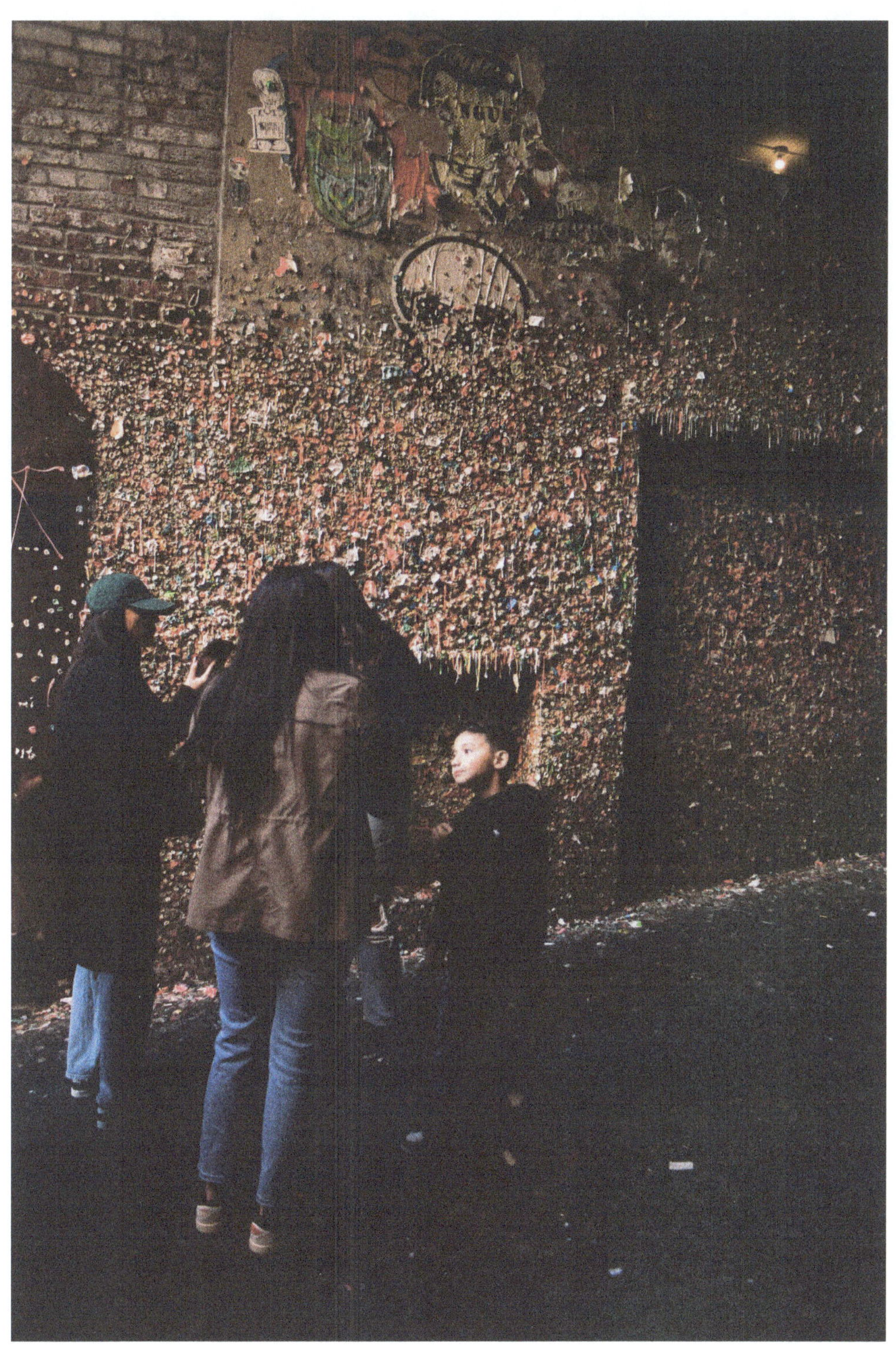

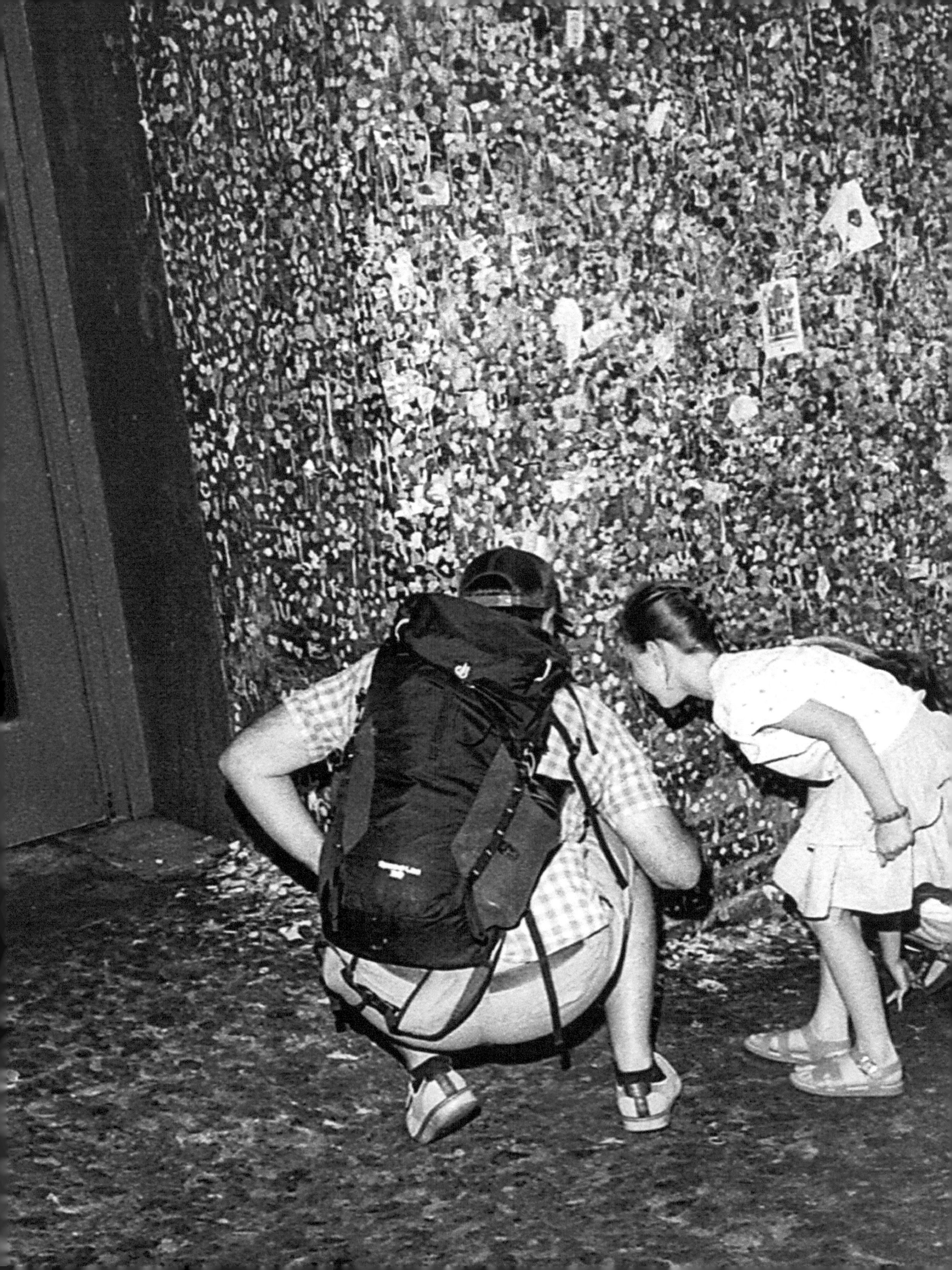

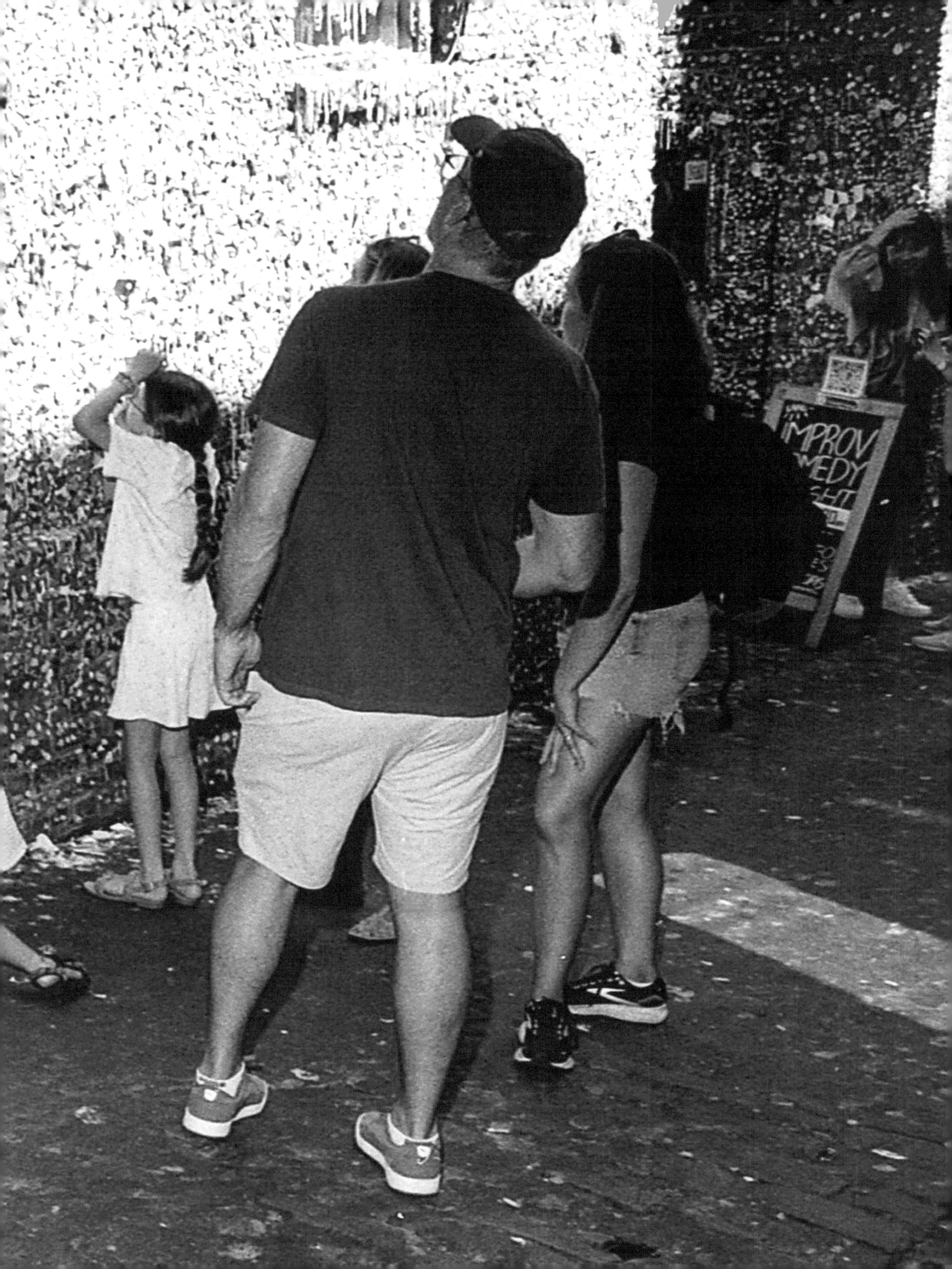

IMPROV
COMEDY
NIGHT

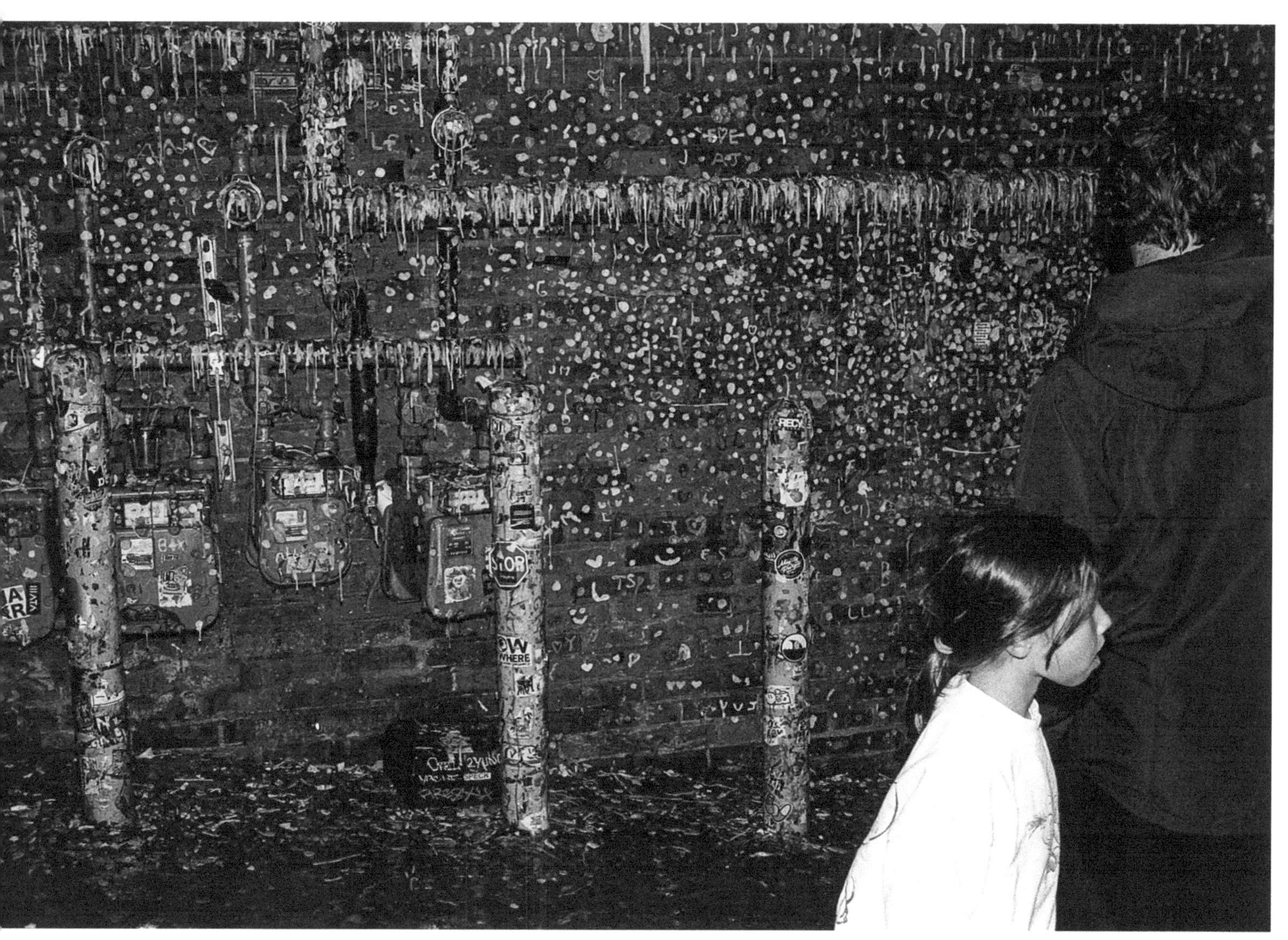

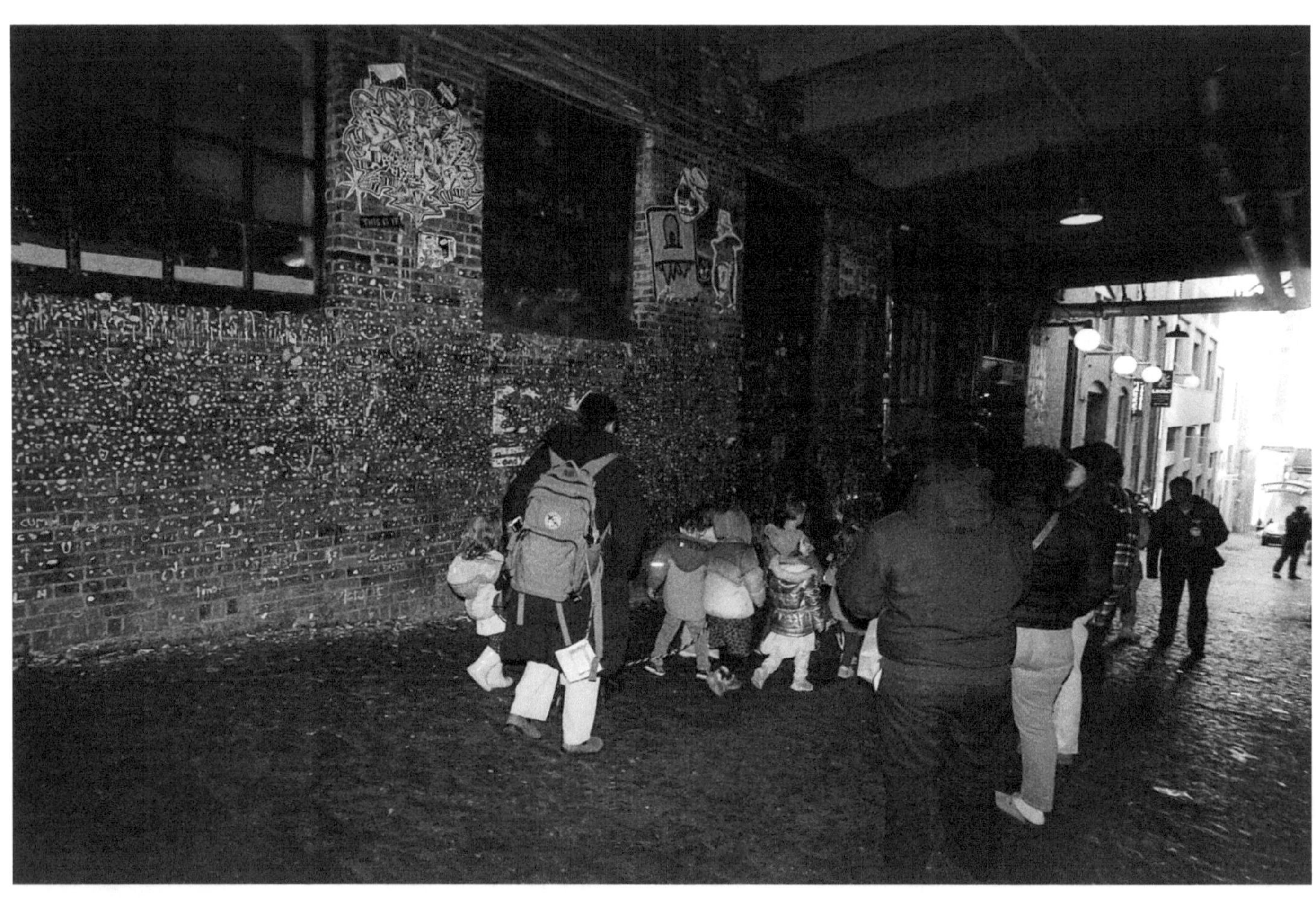

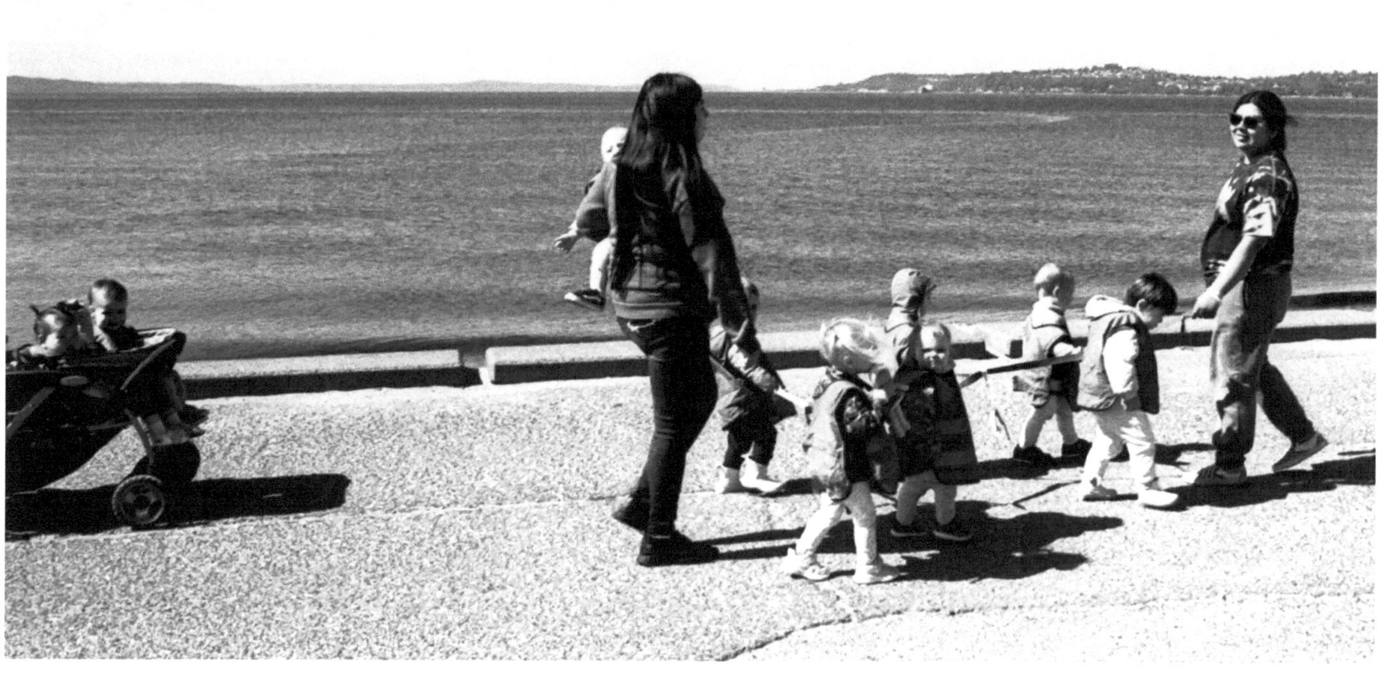

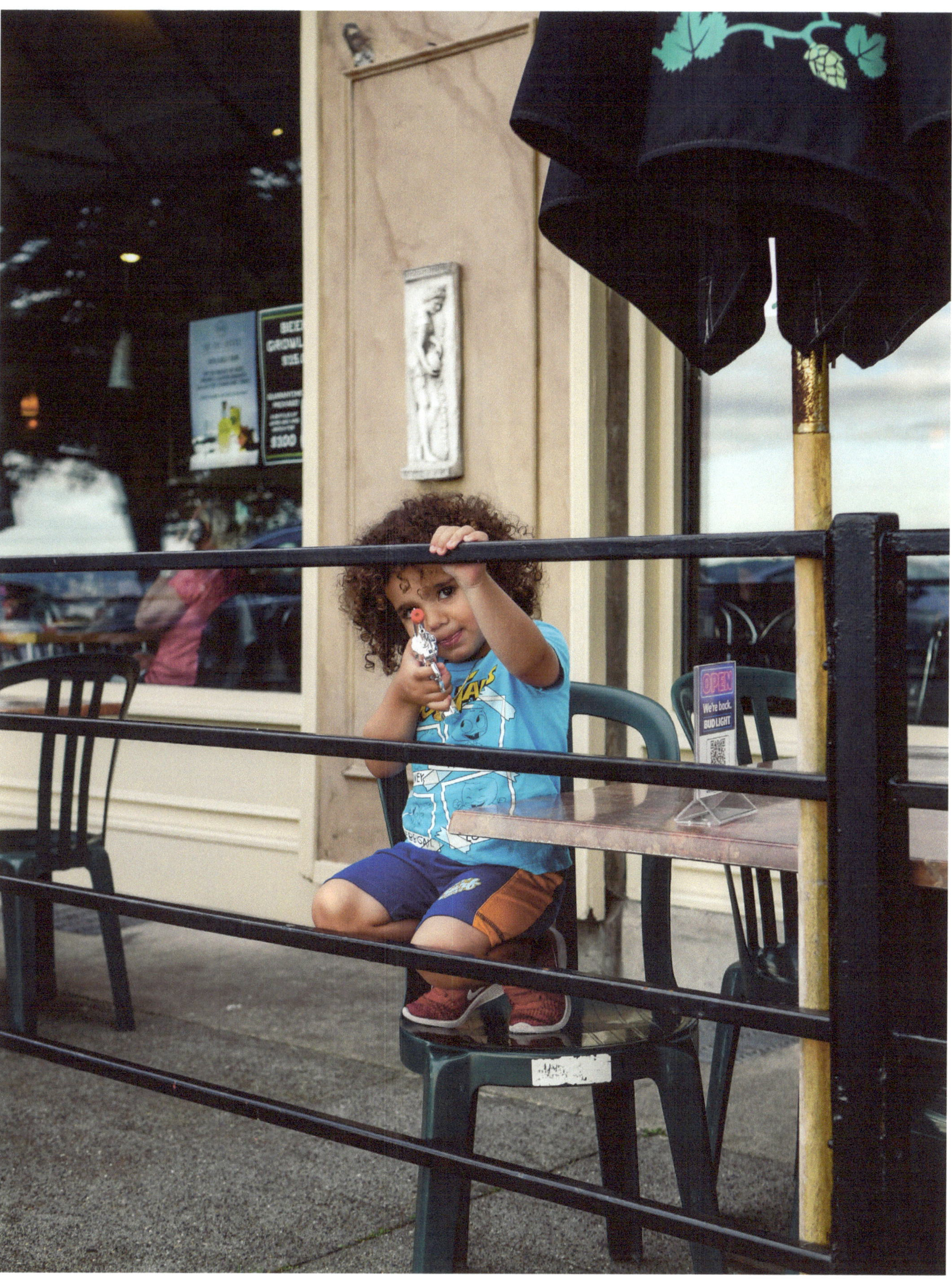
OPEN
We're back.
BUD LIGHT

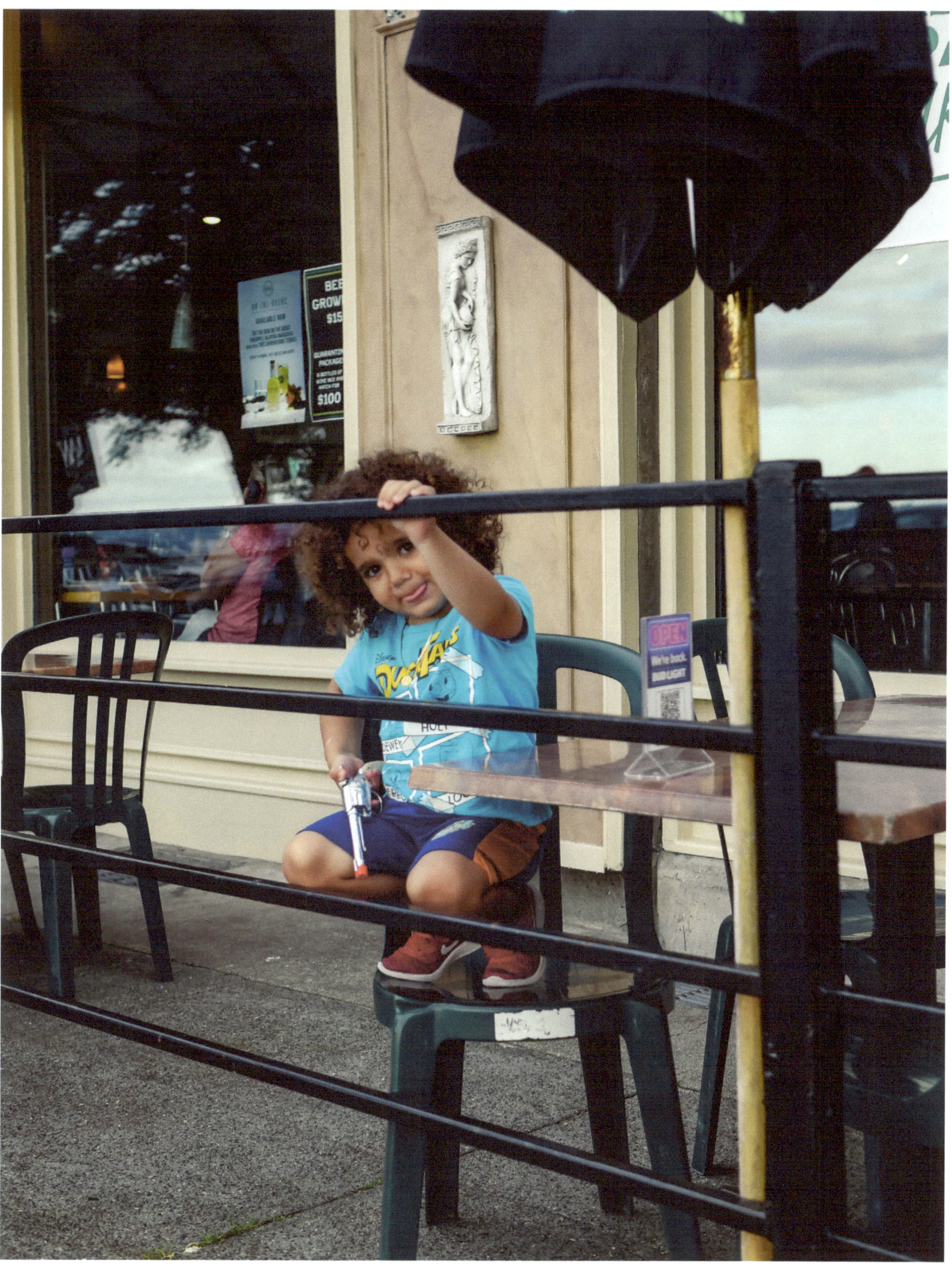

BEE
GROW
$15
$100
OPEN
We're back.
BUD LIGHT

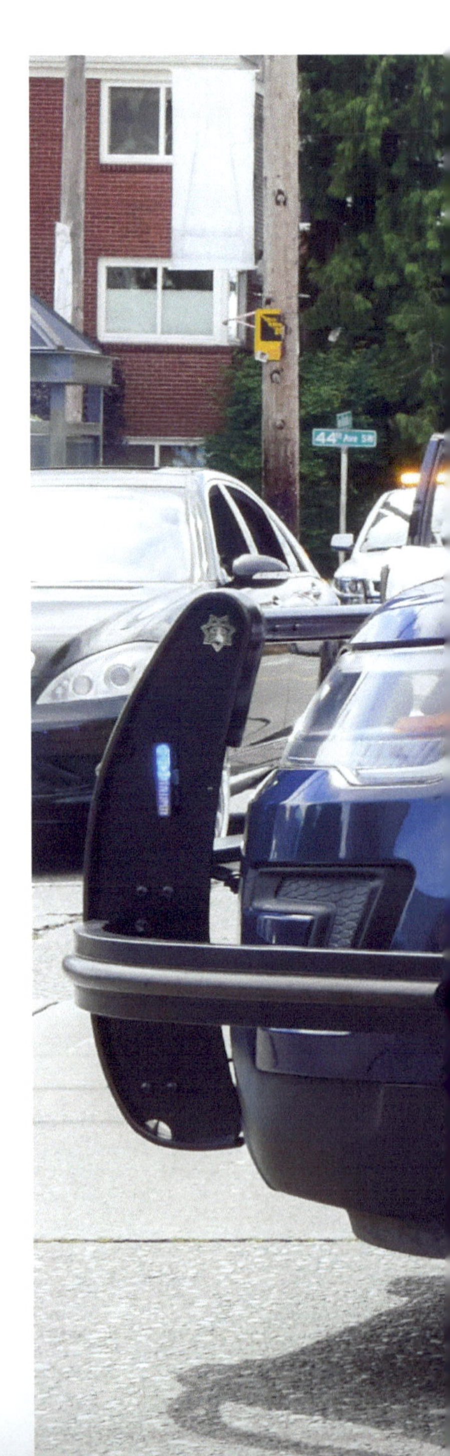
44TH Ave SW

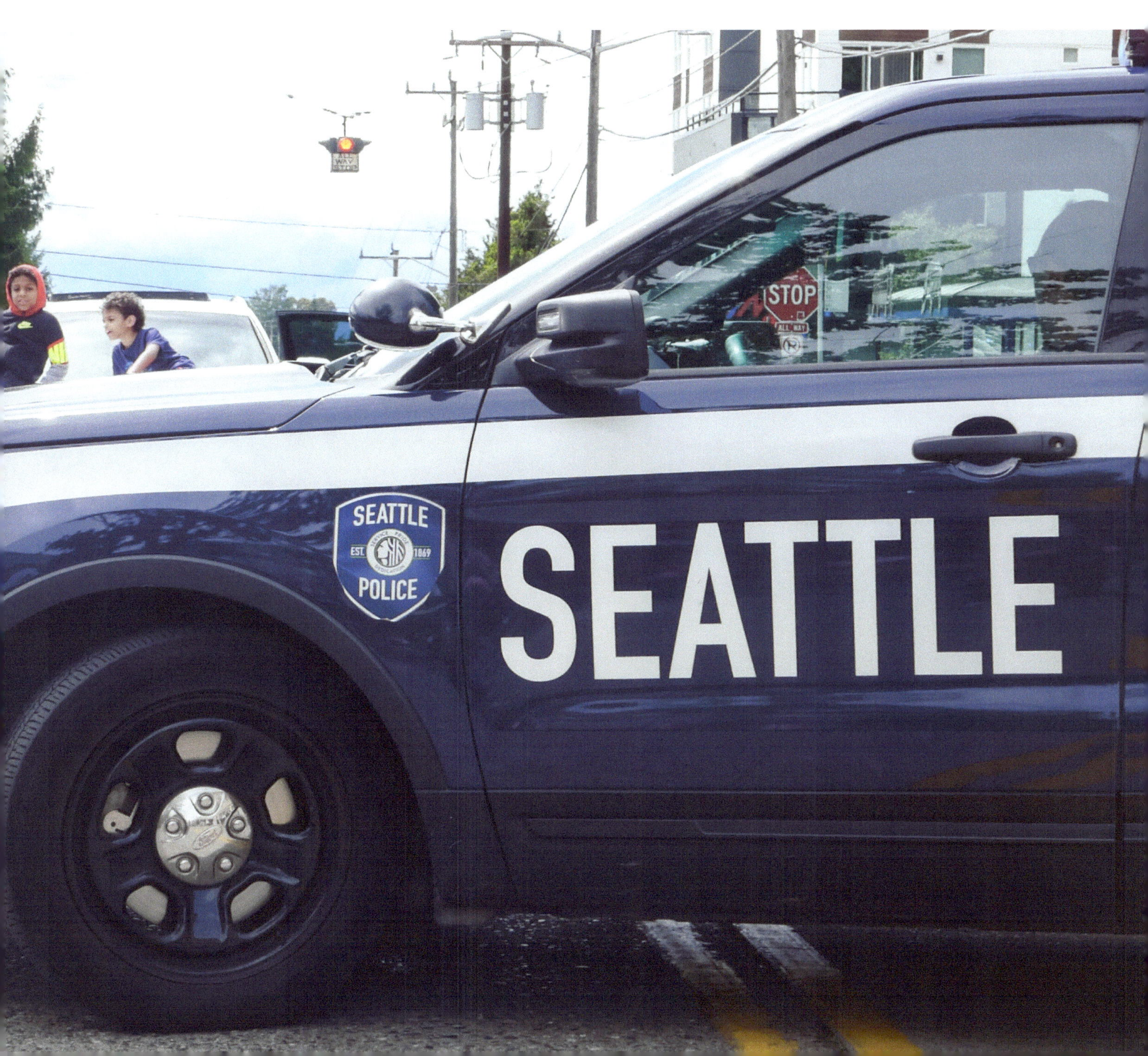

SEATTLE
POLICE
EST. 1869
STOP
ALL WAY
SEATTLE

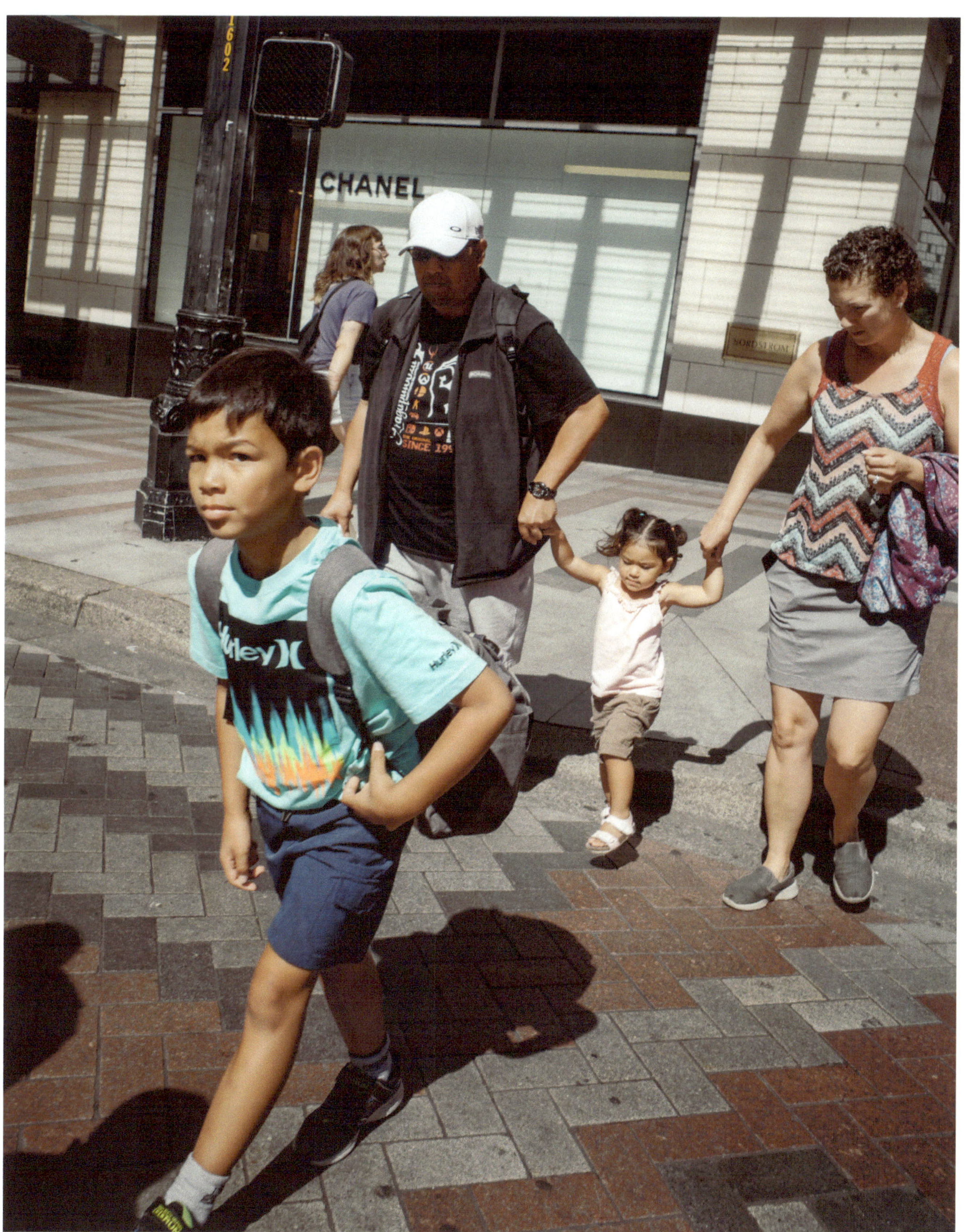
CHANEL
NORDSTROM
Hurley

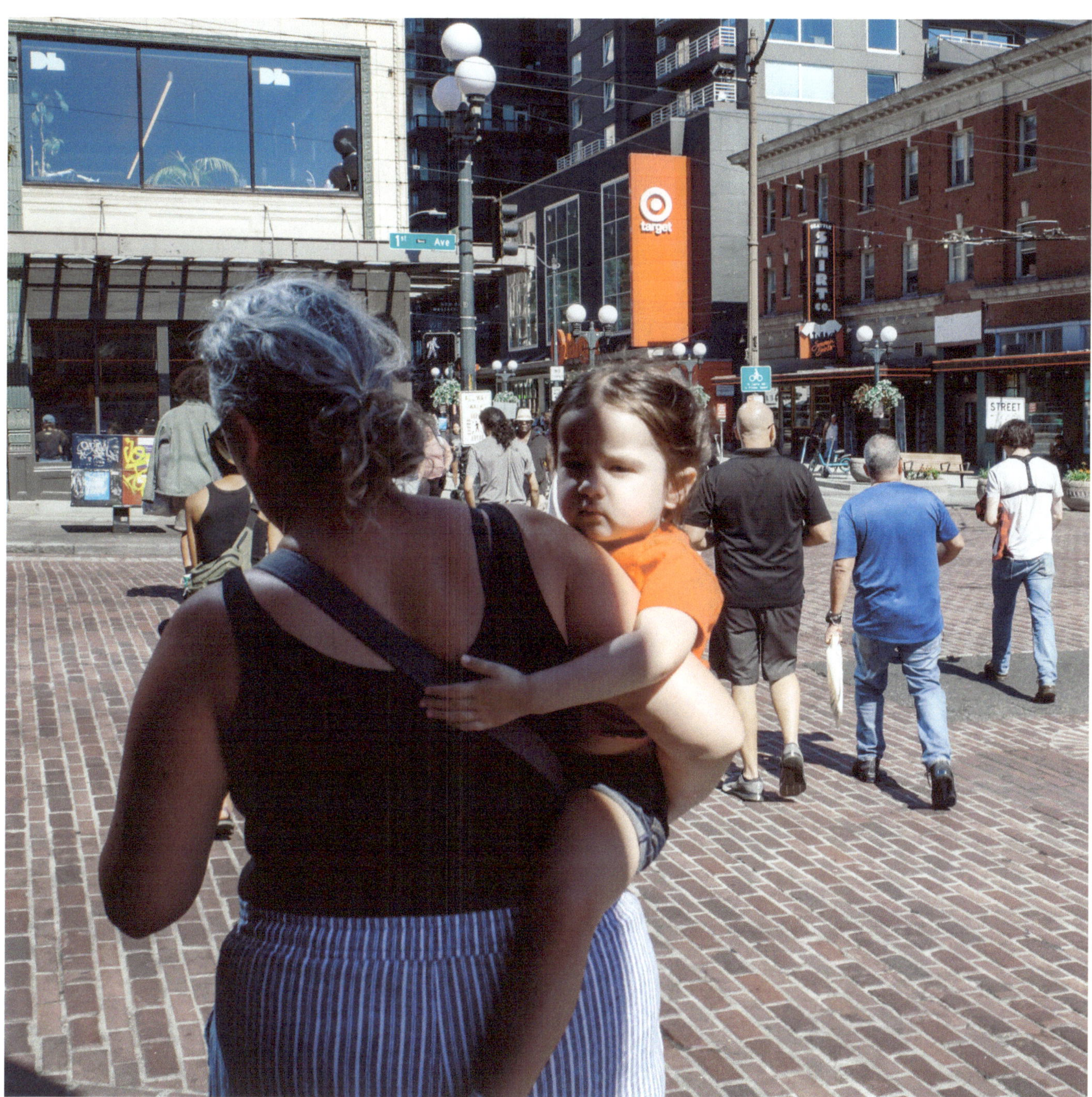

1st Ave
target
SHIRT CO.
STREET

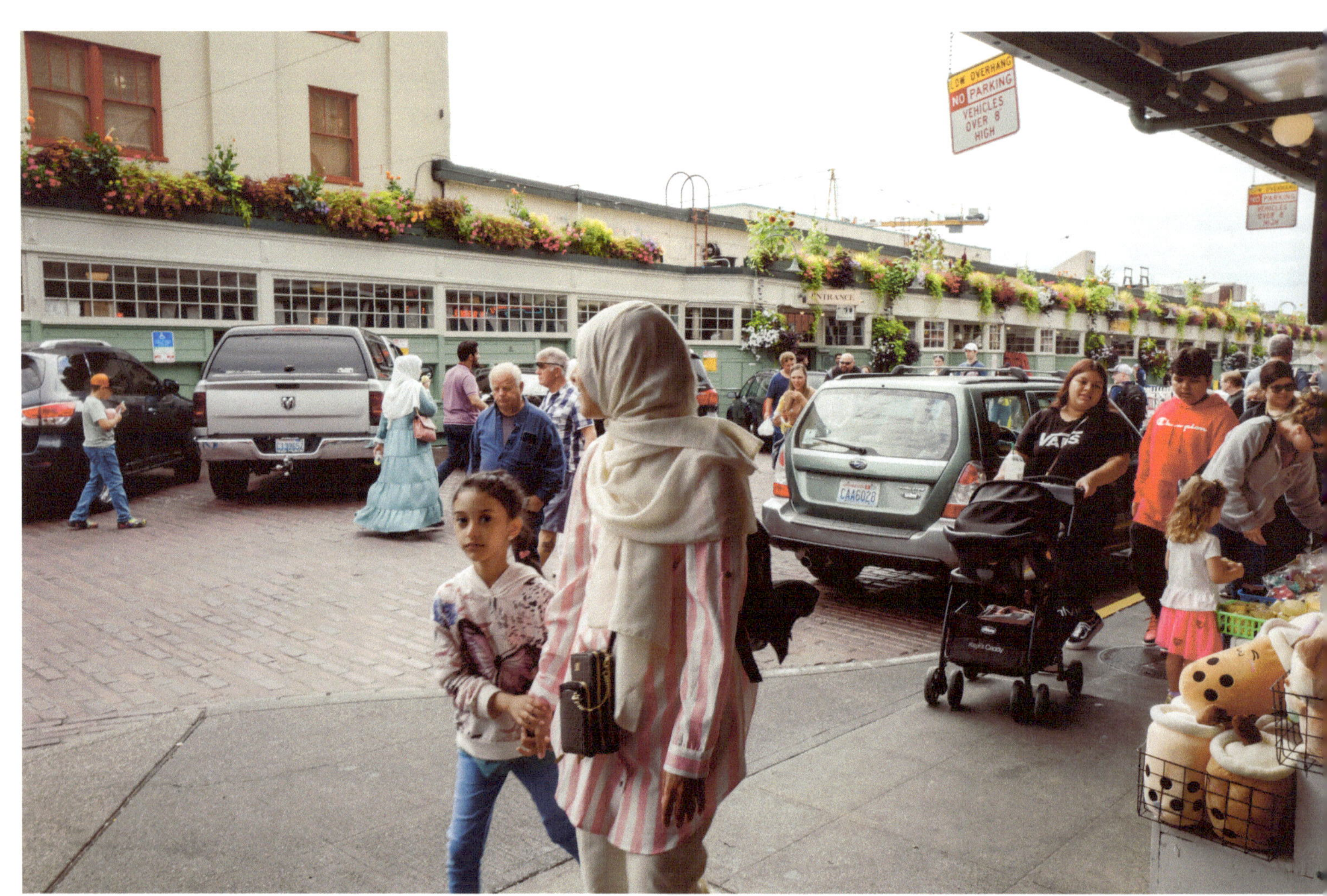

LOW OVERHANG
NO PARKING
VEHICLES
OVER 8'
HIGH
ENTRANCE
VANS
CAA6028

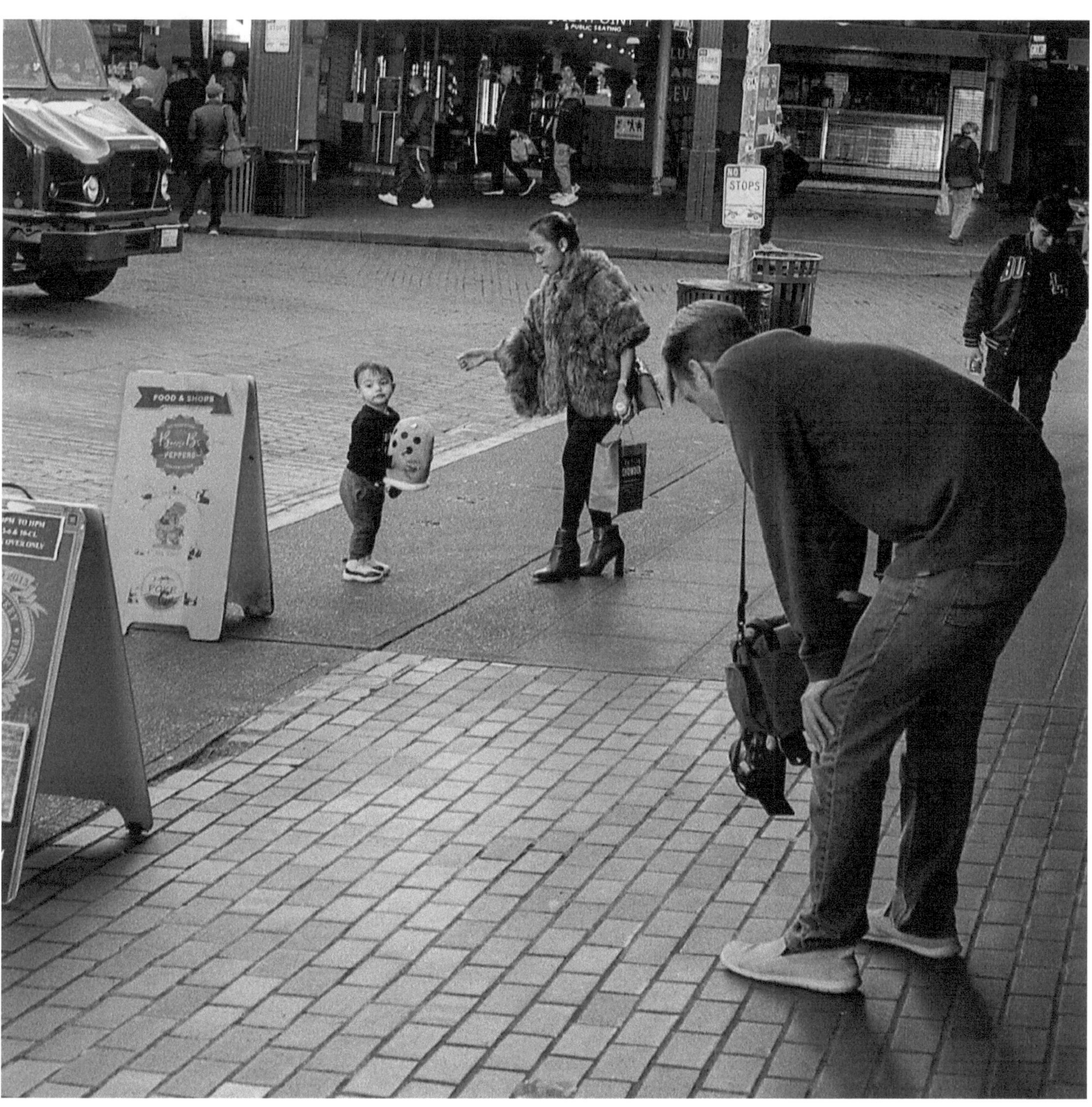

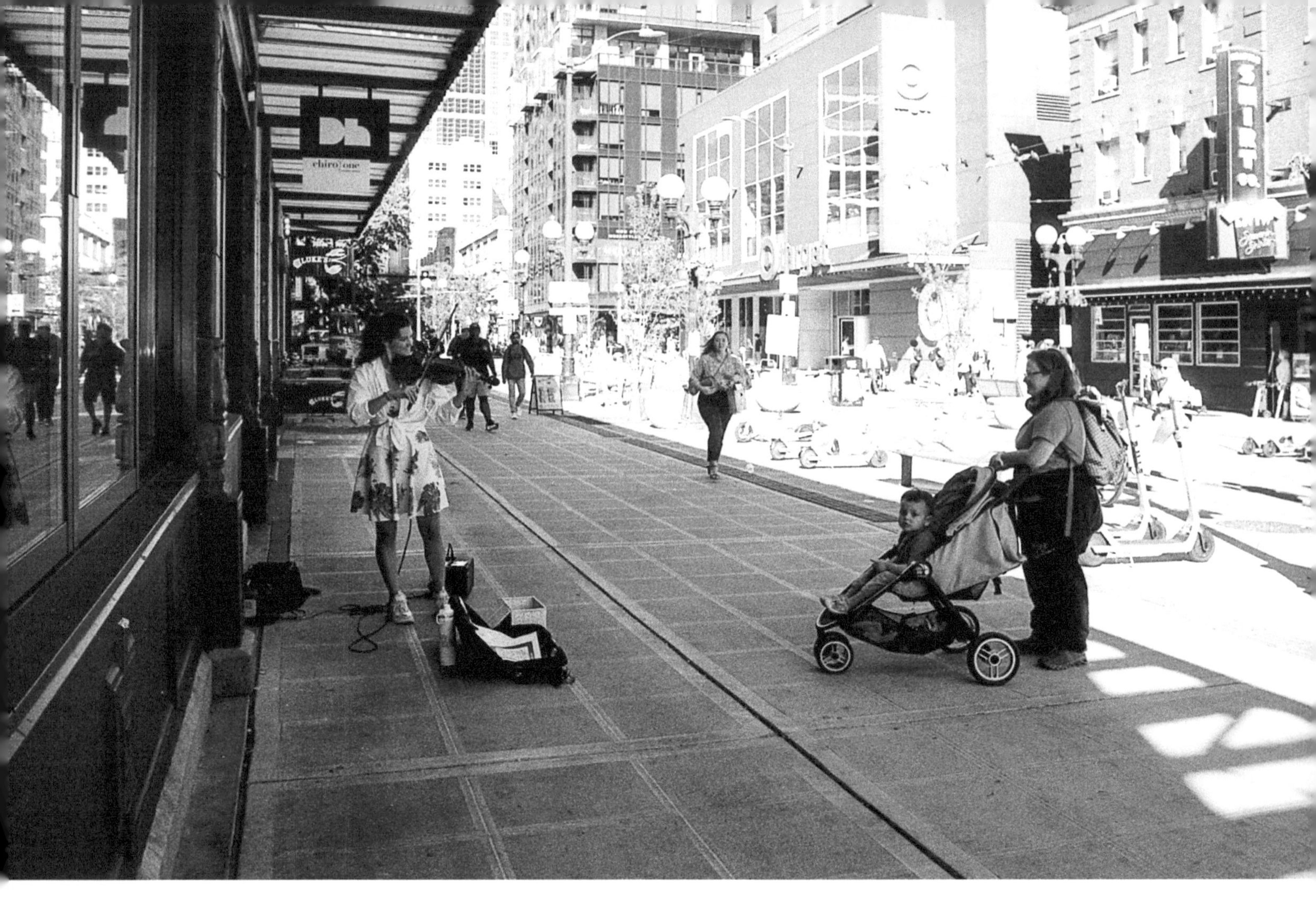

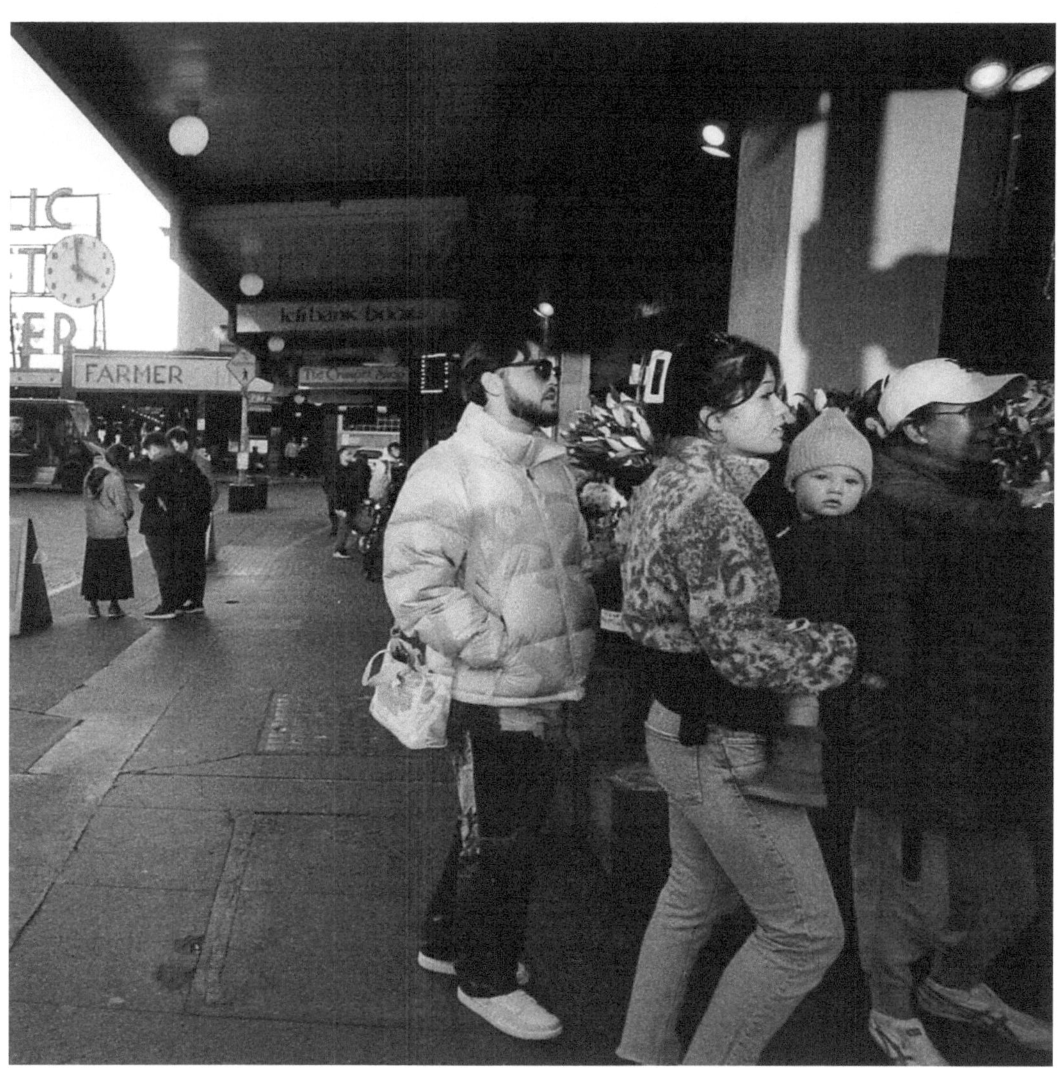

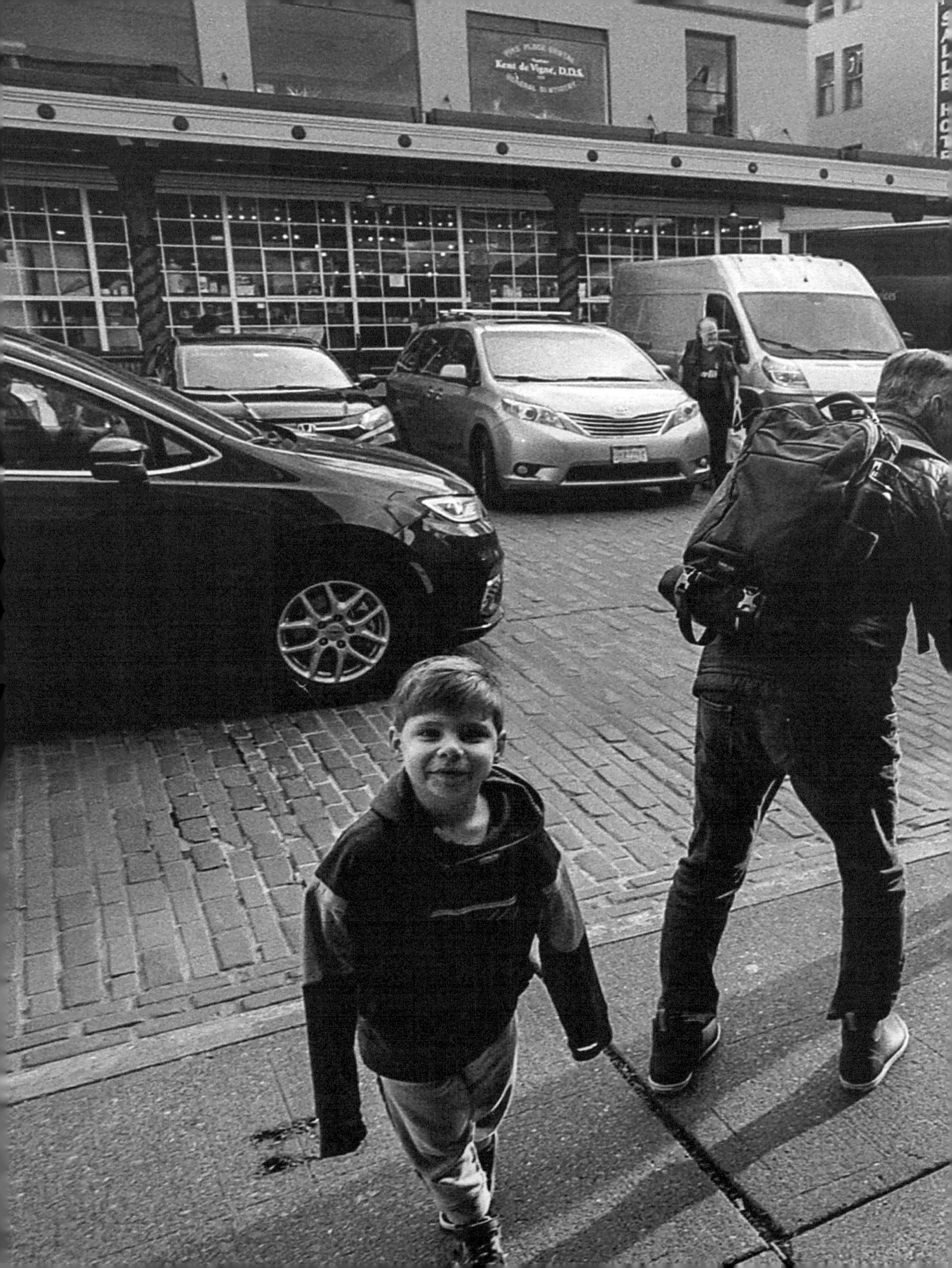

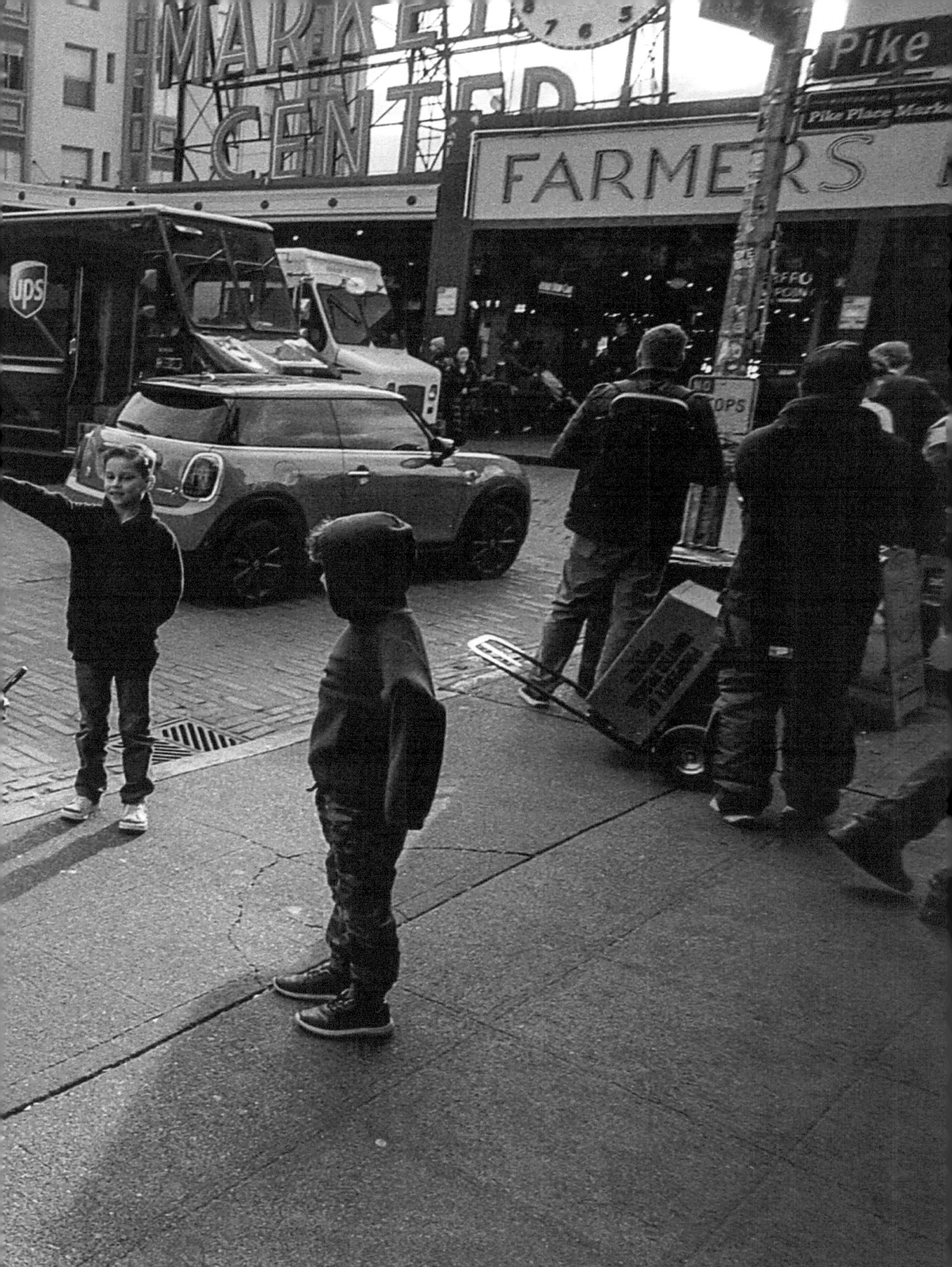
MARKET
CENTER
Pike
Pike Place Market
FARMERS
UPS

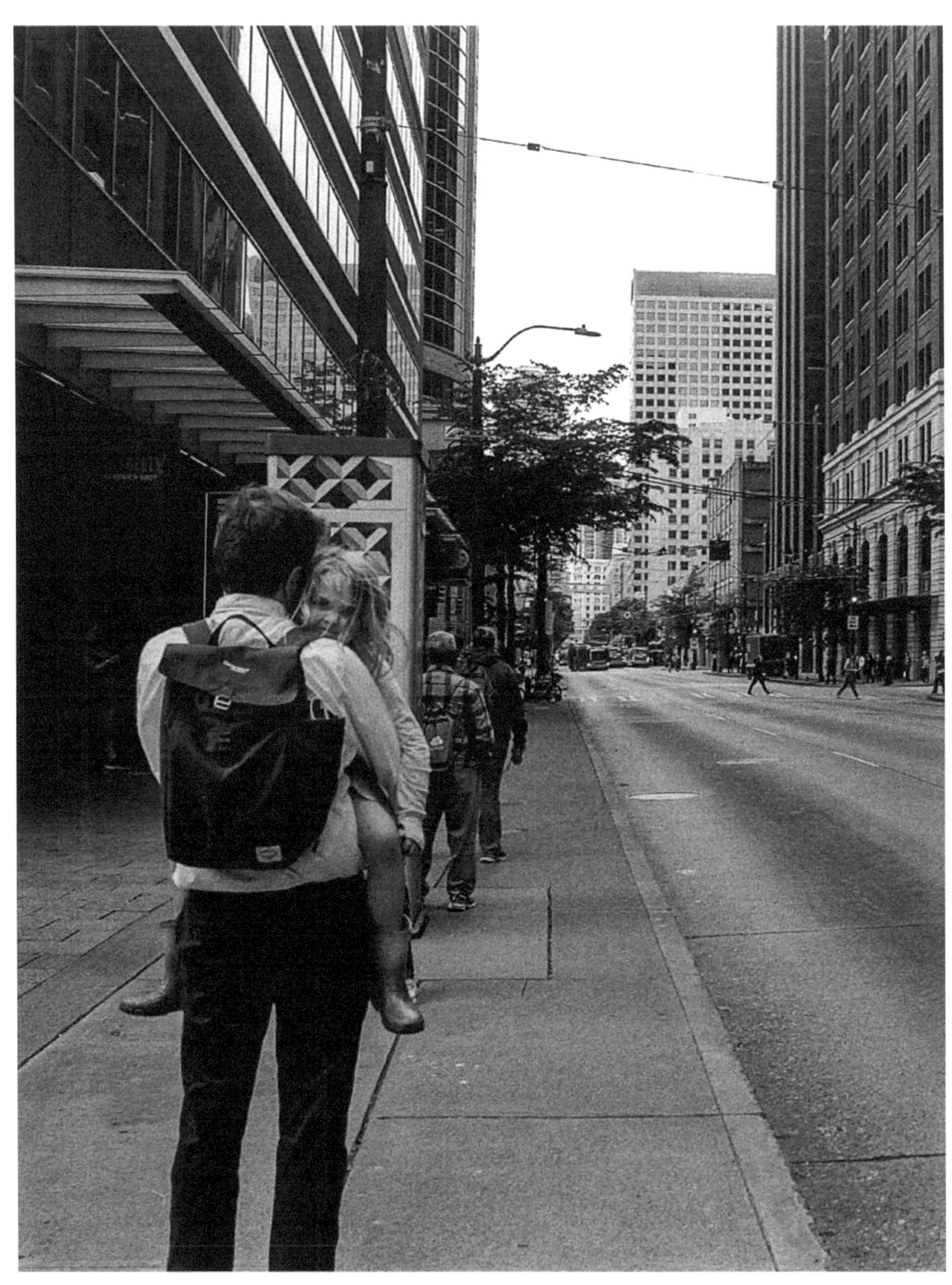

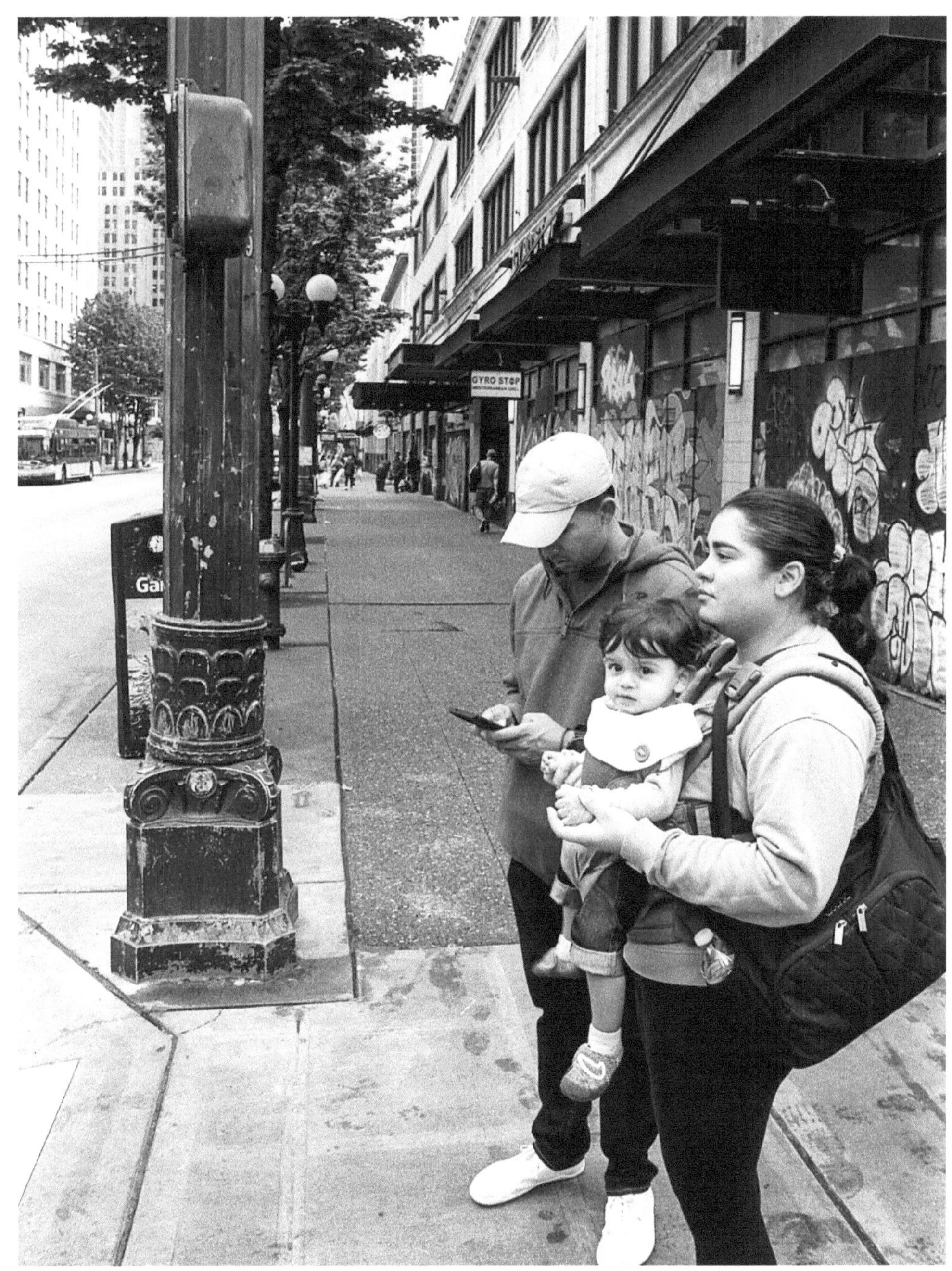
GYRO STOP

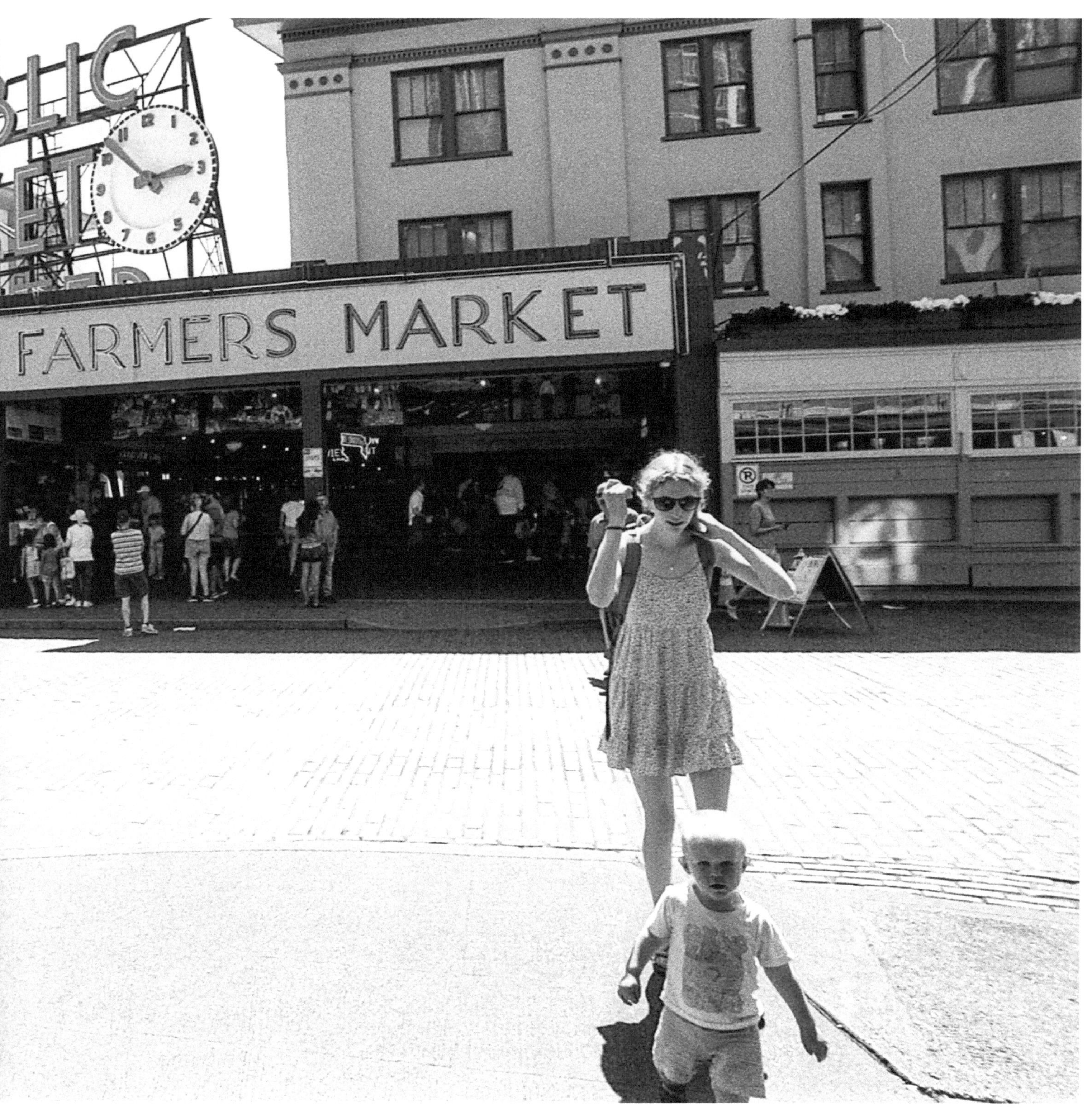
LIC
ET
FARMERS MARKET

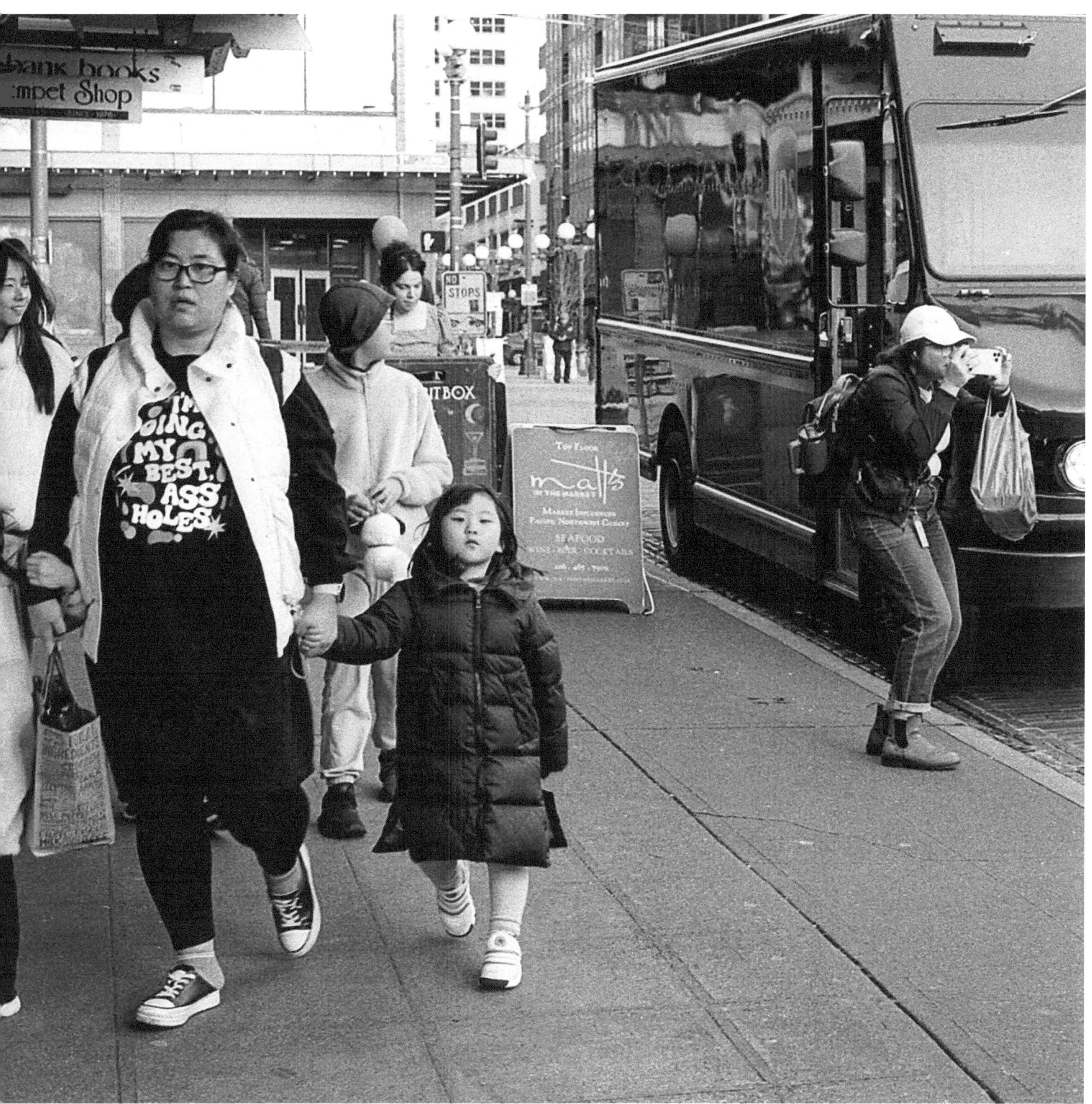

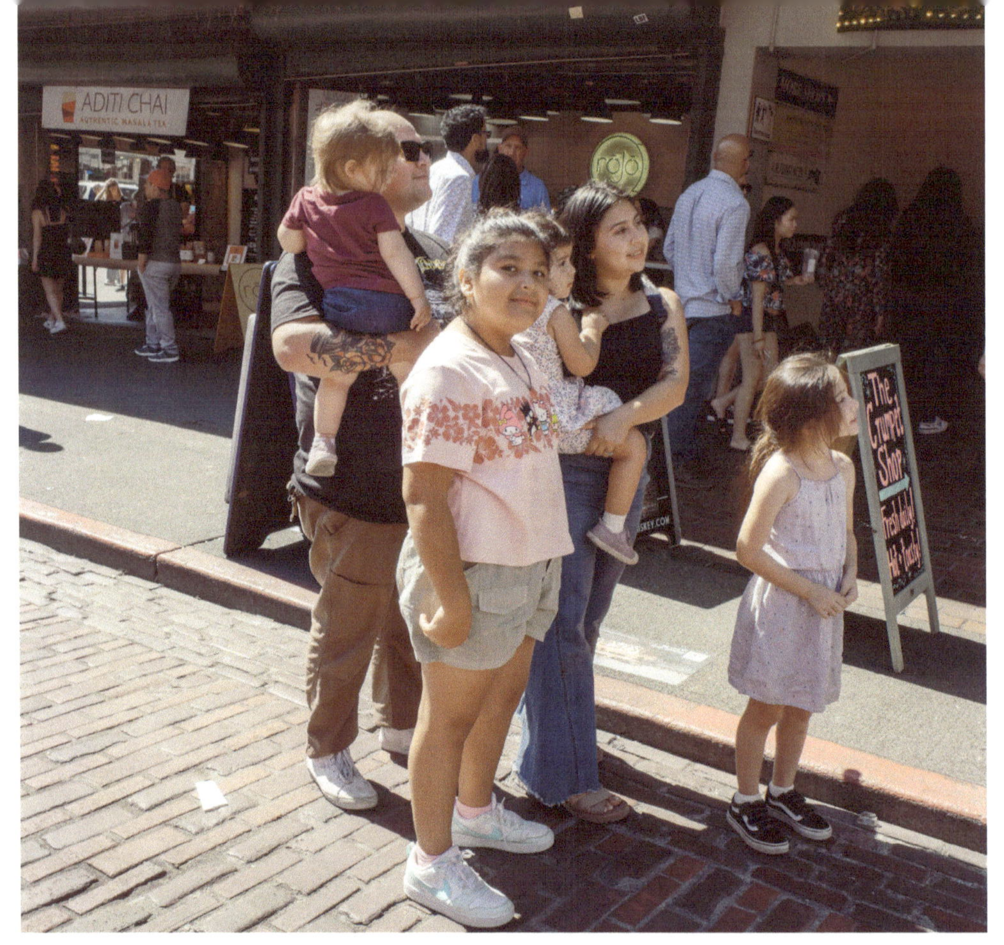
ADITI CHAI
AUTHENTIC MASALA TEA
The Crumpet Shop
Fresh daily!
Hot + Toasty!

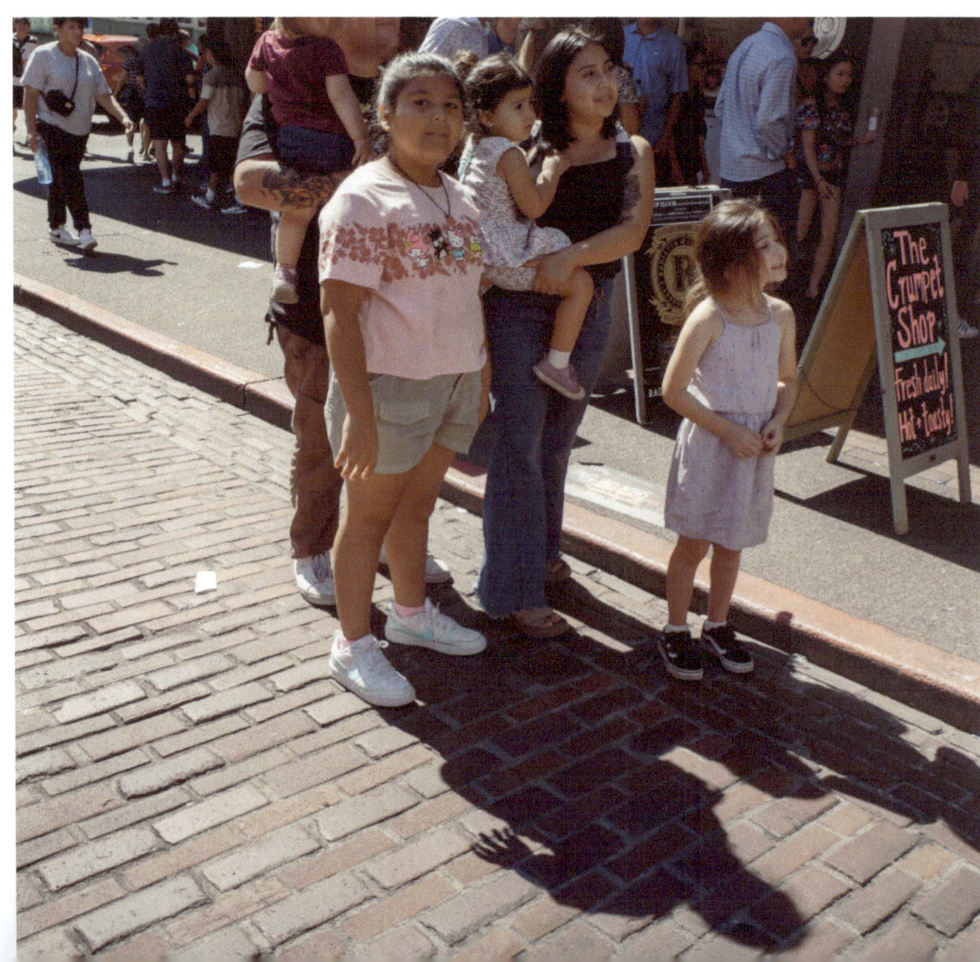
The Crumpet Shop
Fresh daily!
Hot + Toasty!

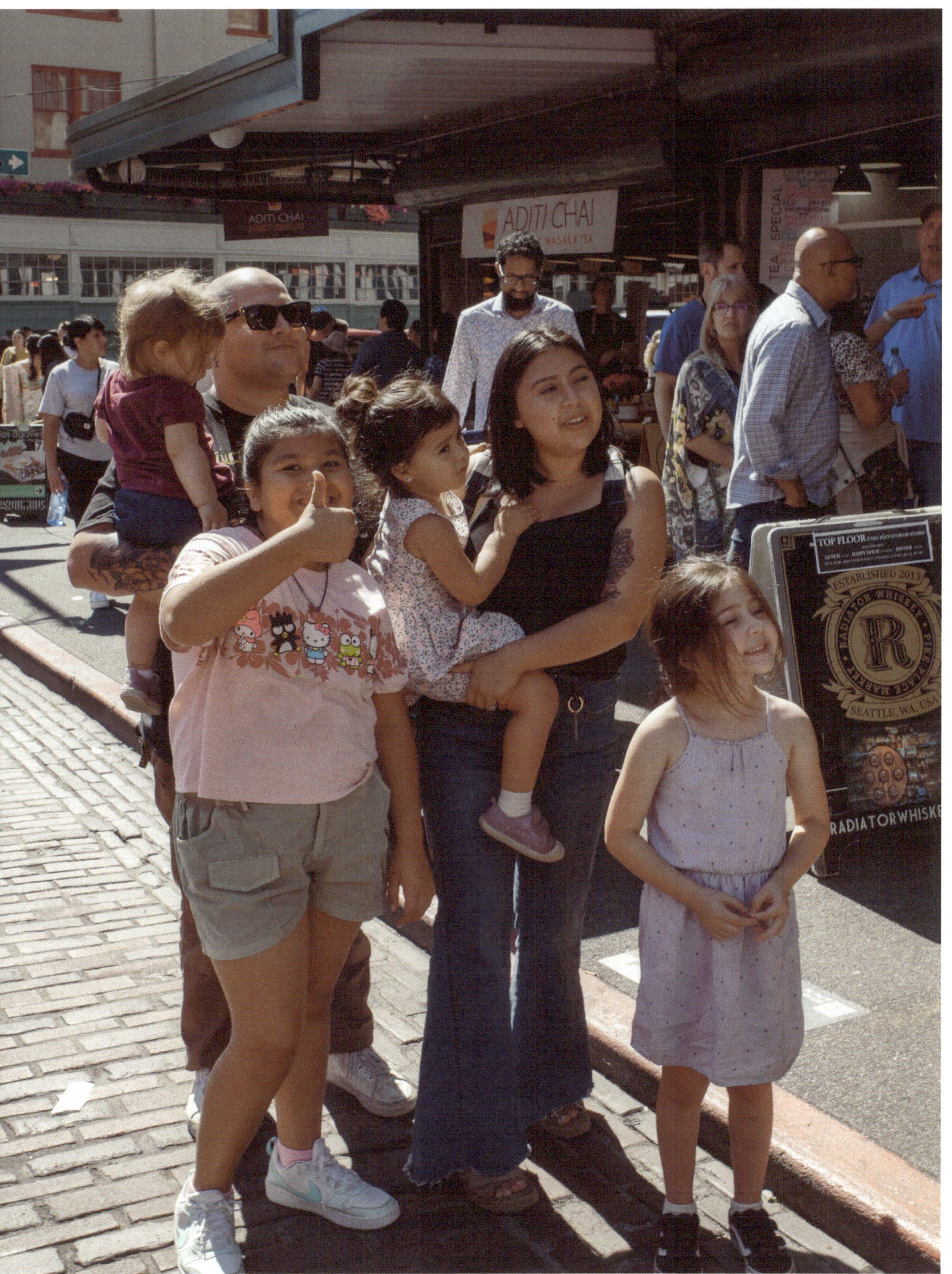

ADITI CHAI
ADITI CHAI
MASALA TEA
TEA SPECIAL
TOP FLOOR
ESTABLISHED 2013
RADIATOR WHISKEY
R
SEATTLE, WA, USA
RADIATORWHISKE

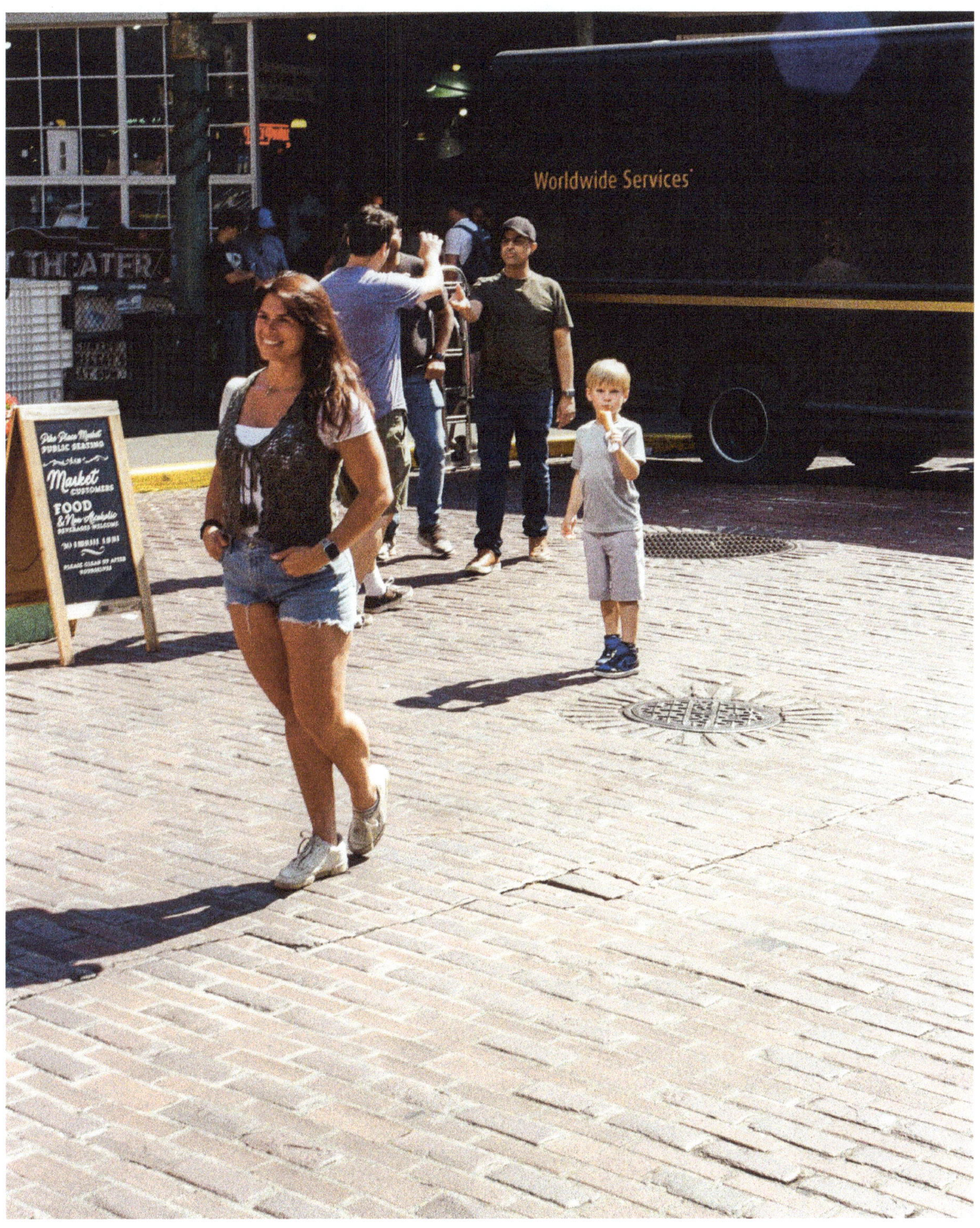

Worldwide Services
THEATER
Pike Place Market
PUBLIC SEATING
Market
CUSTOMERS
FOOD
& Non Alcoholic
BEVERAGES WELCOME

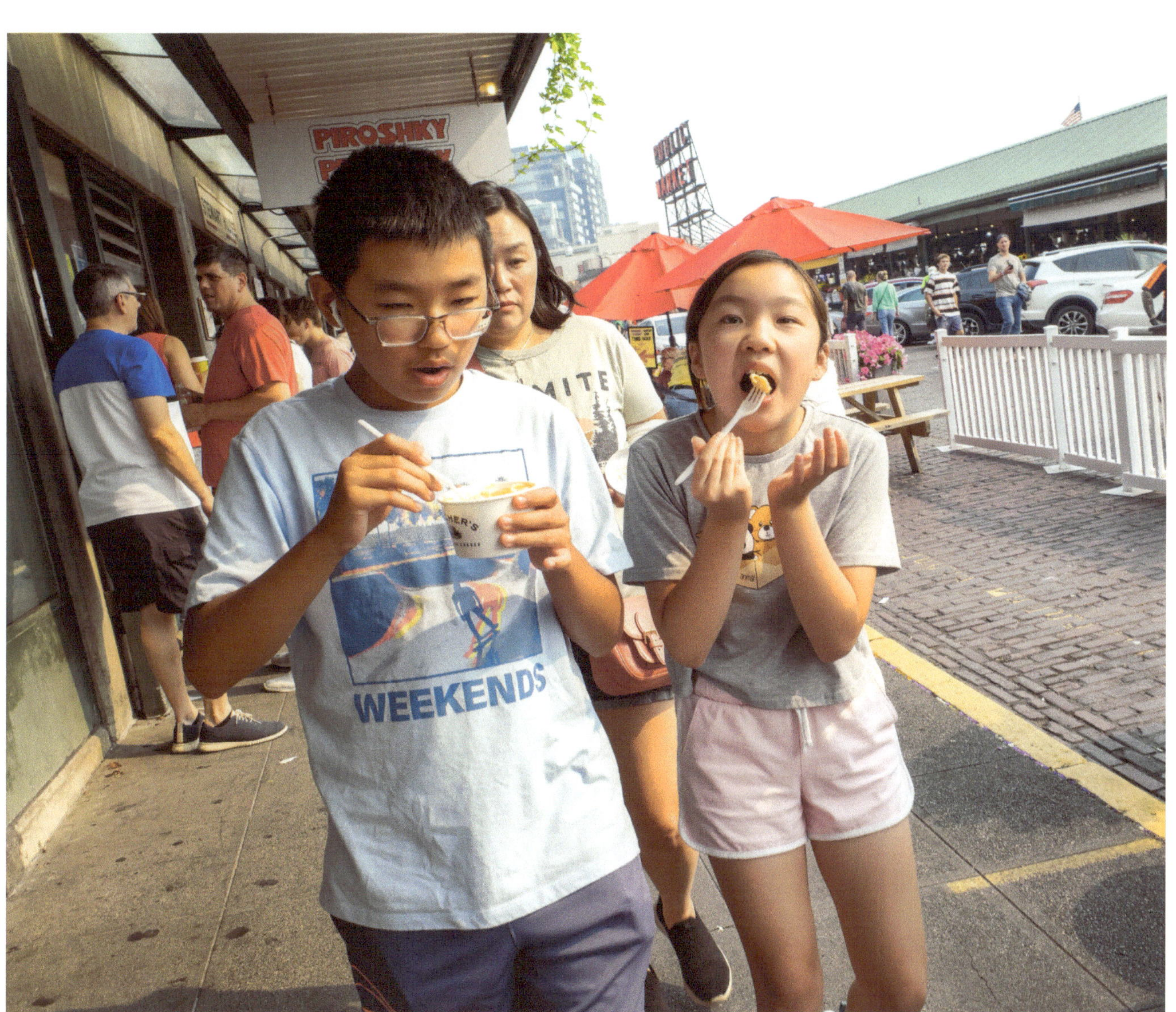

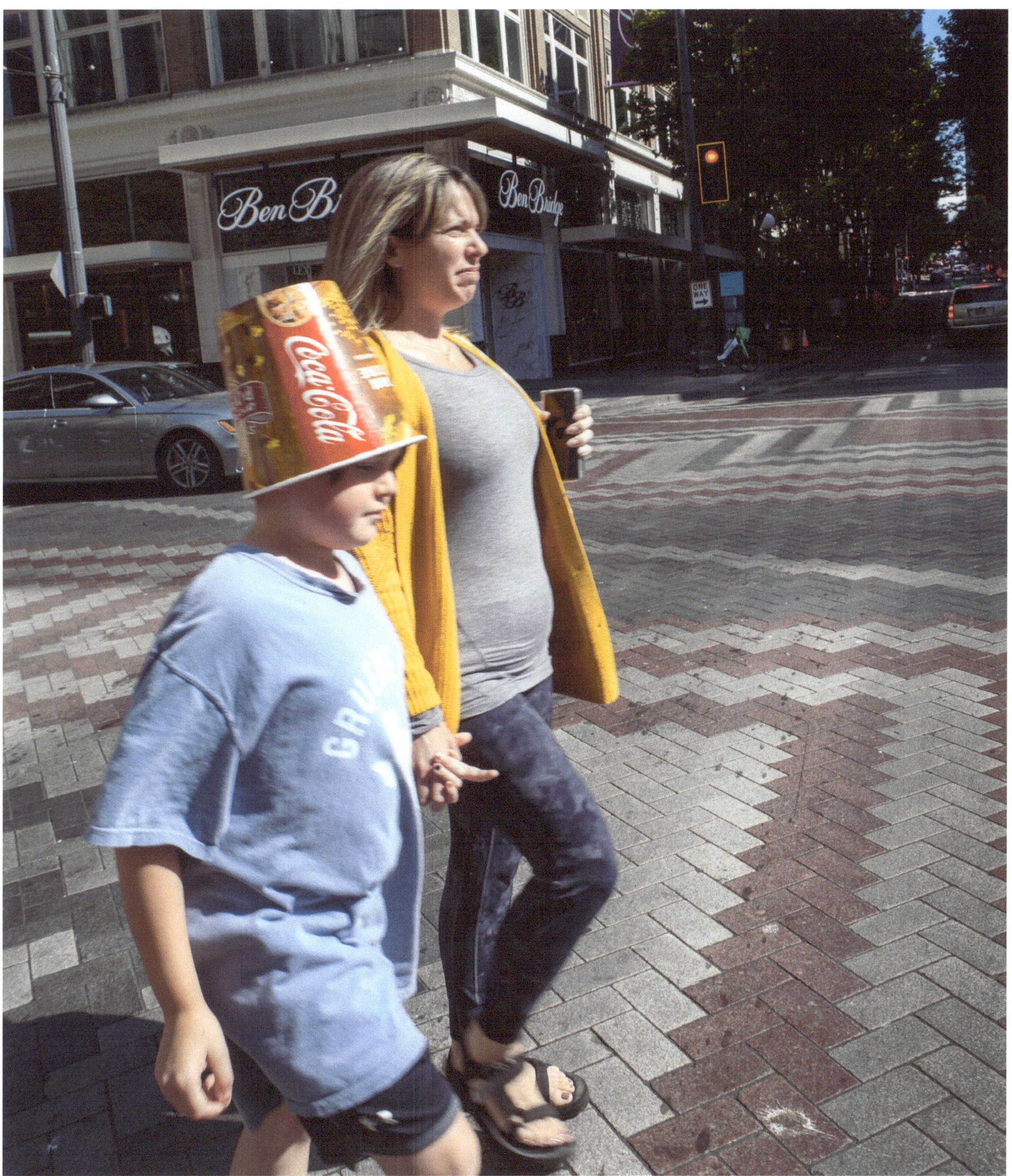

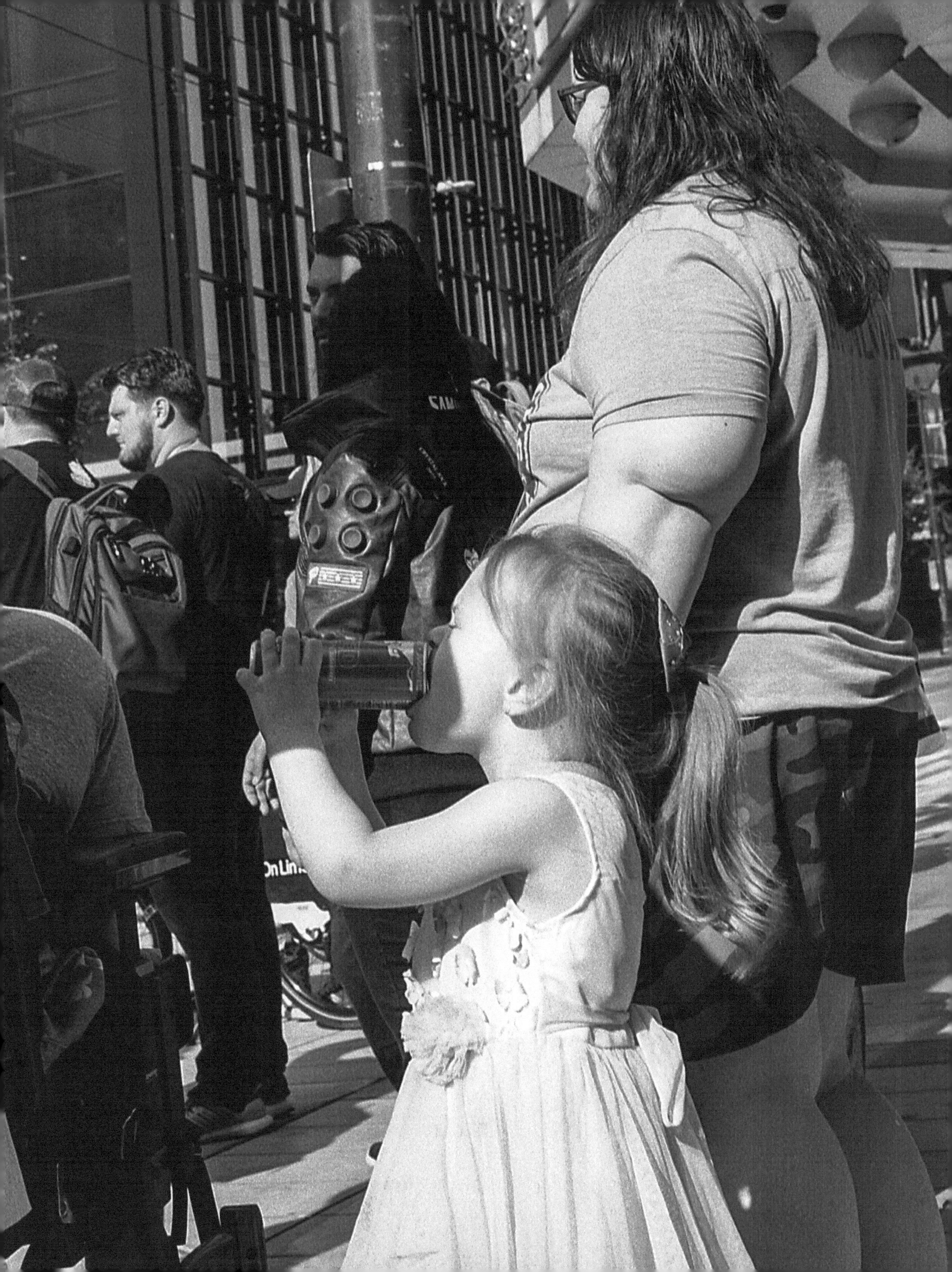

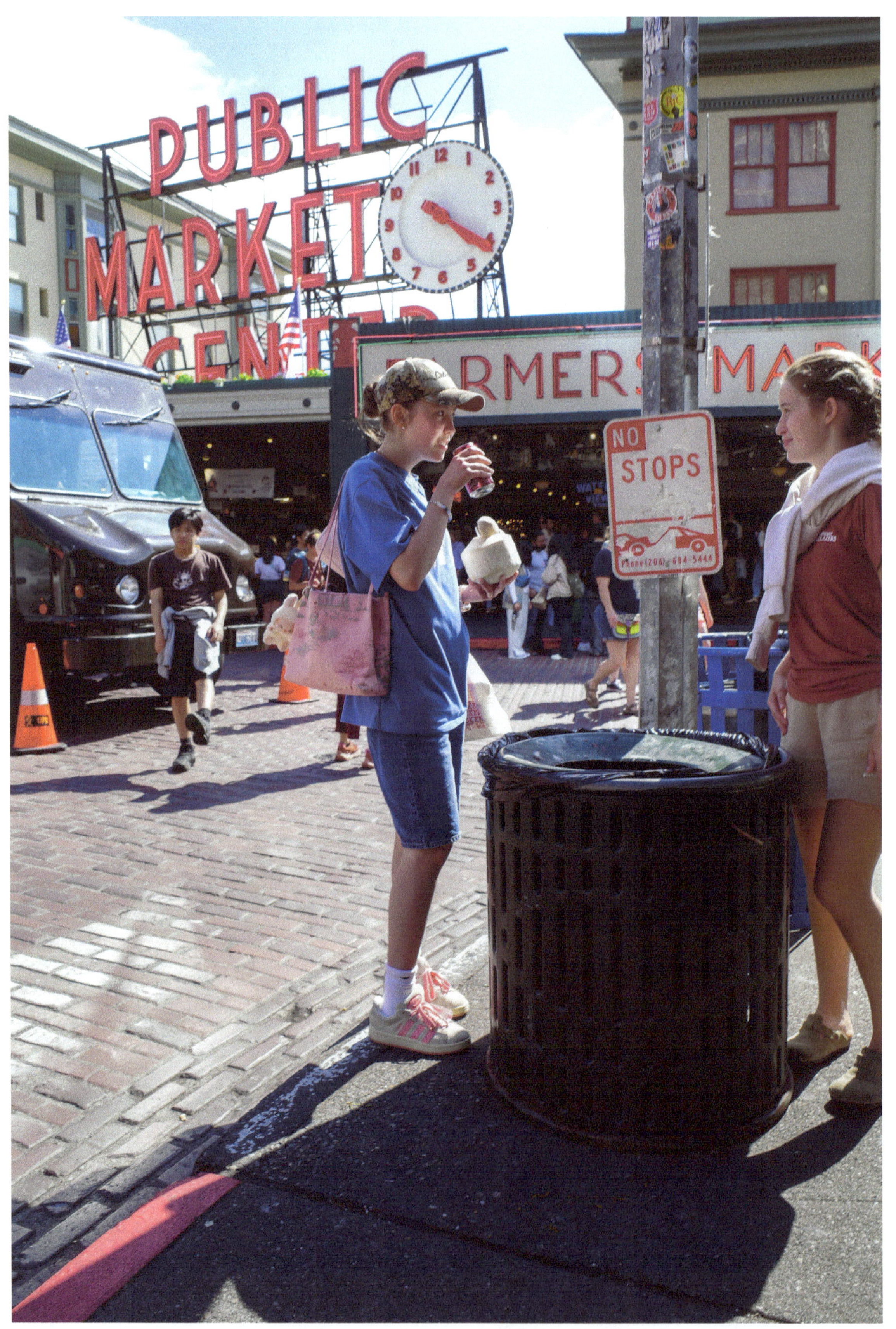
PUBLIC
MARKET
CENTER
FARMERS MARKET
NO
STOPS

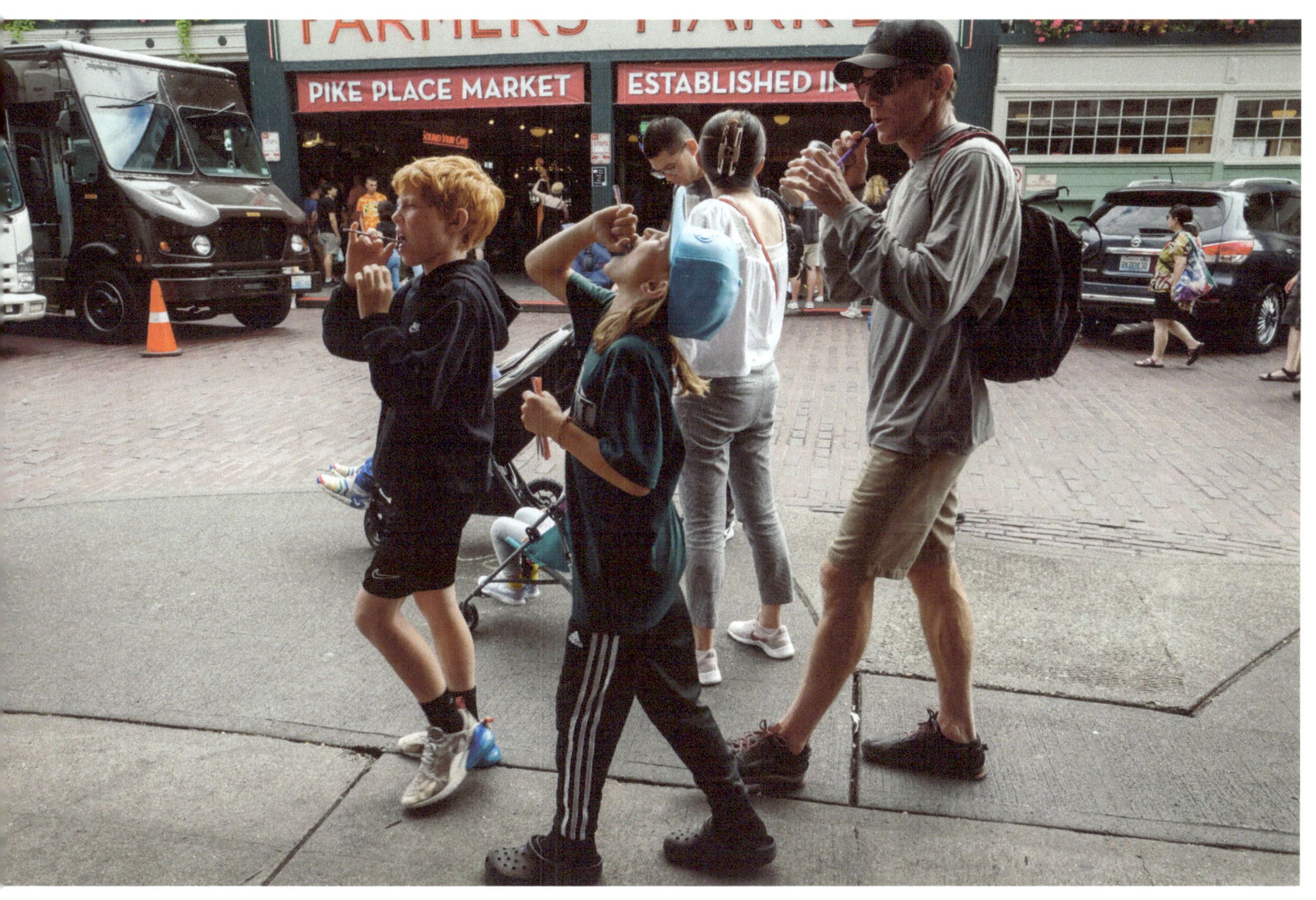

FARMERS MARKET
PIKE PLACE MARKET
ESTABLISHED IN

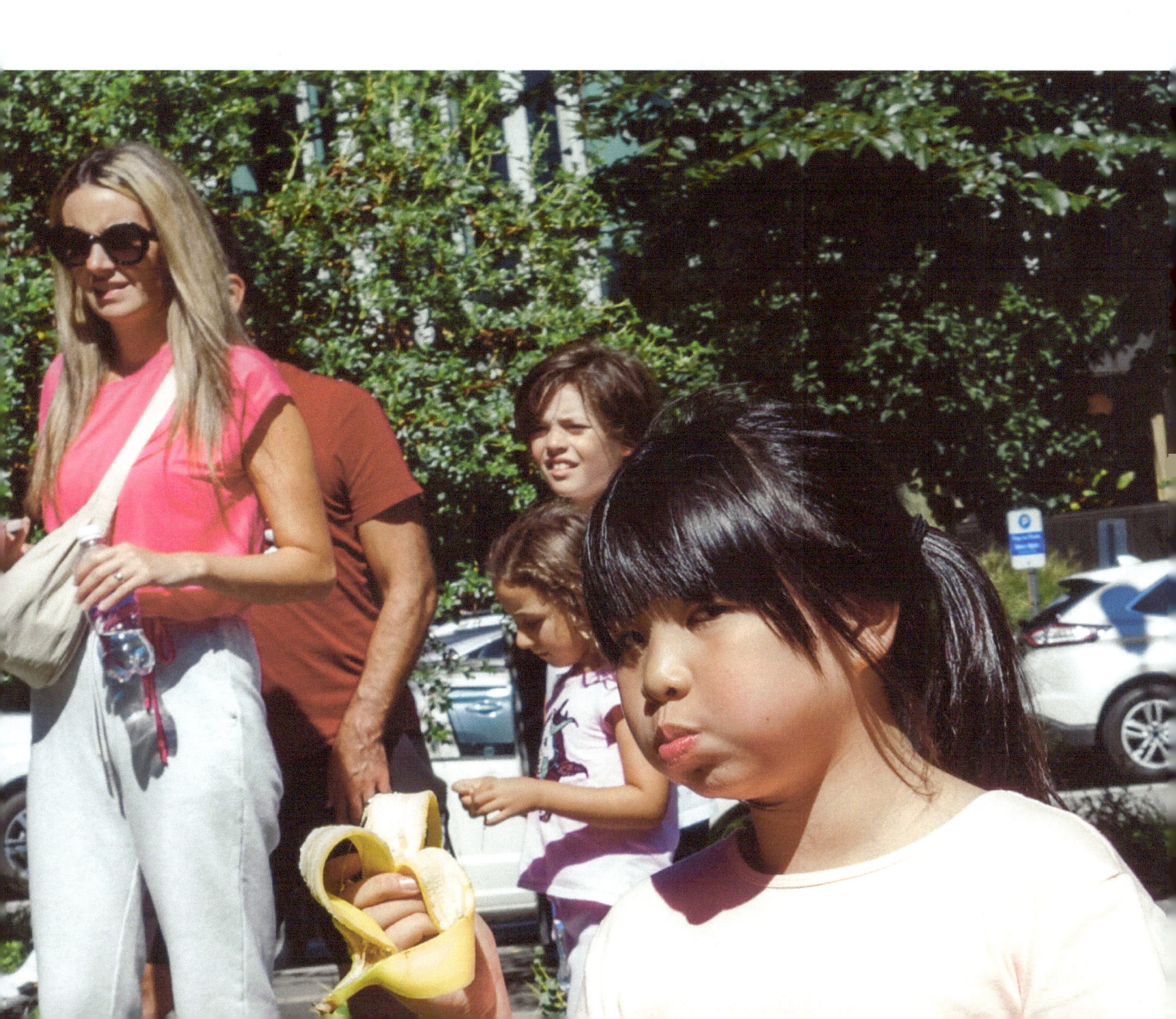

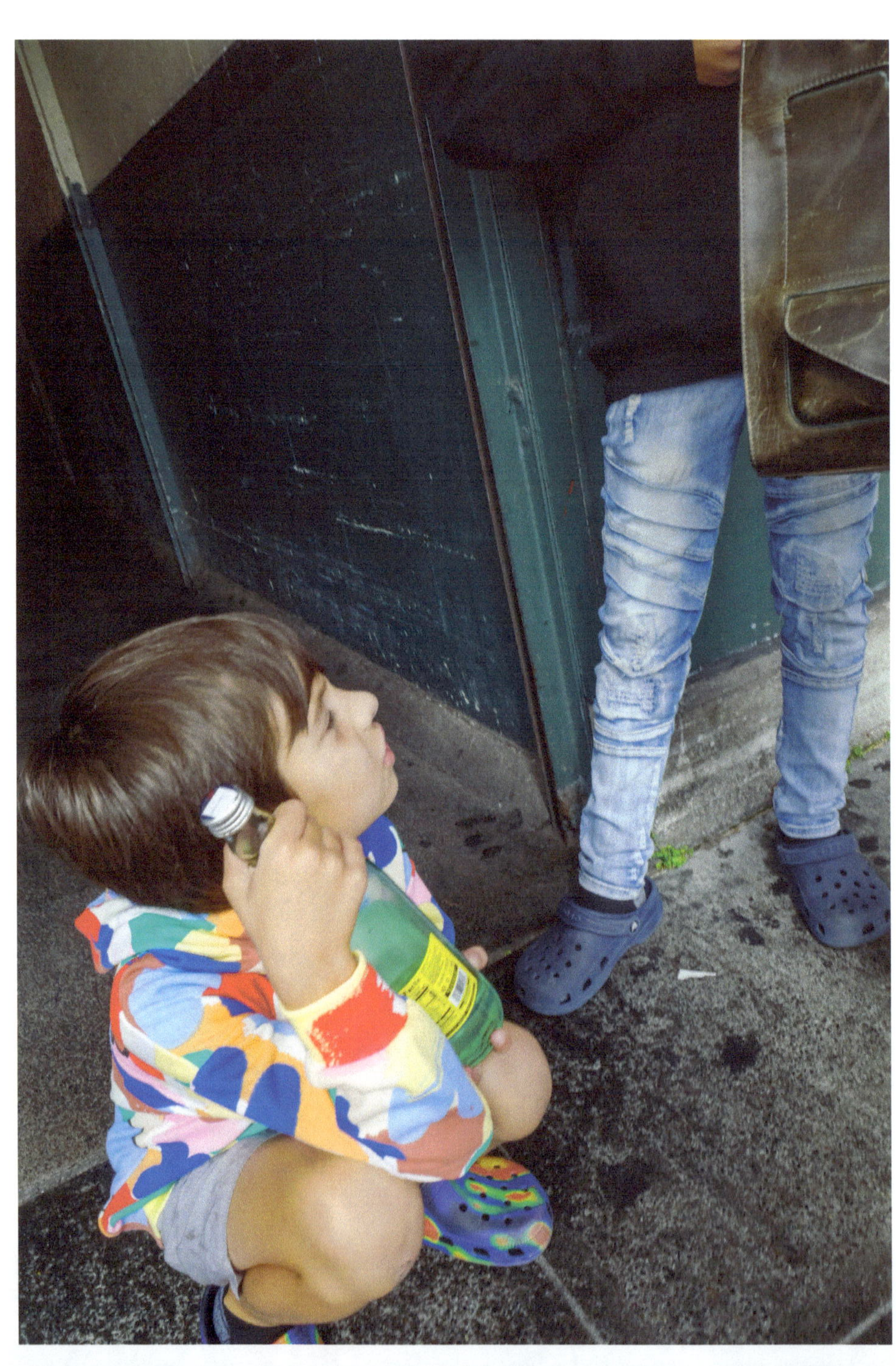

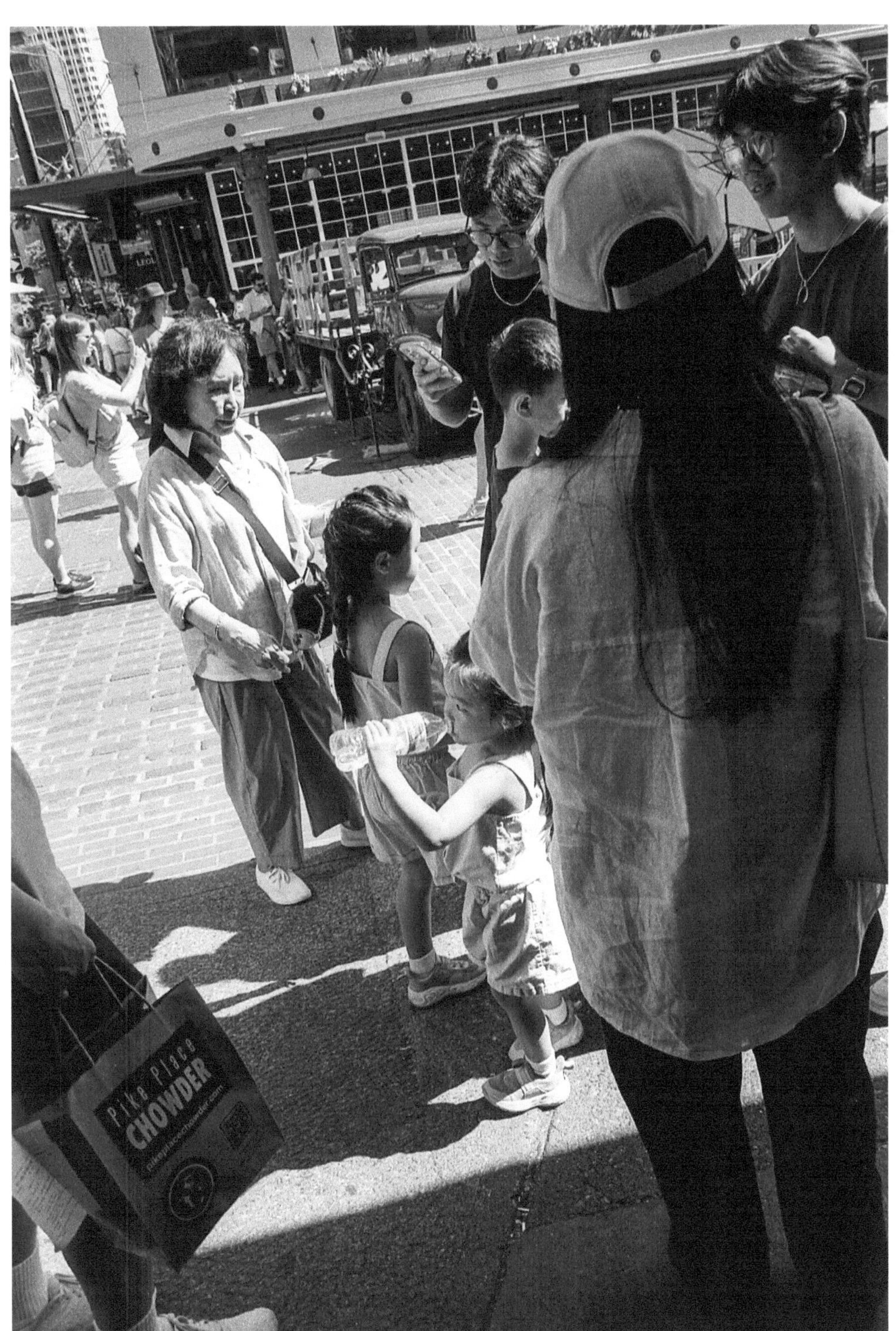

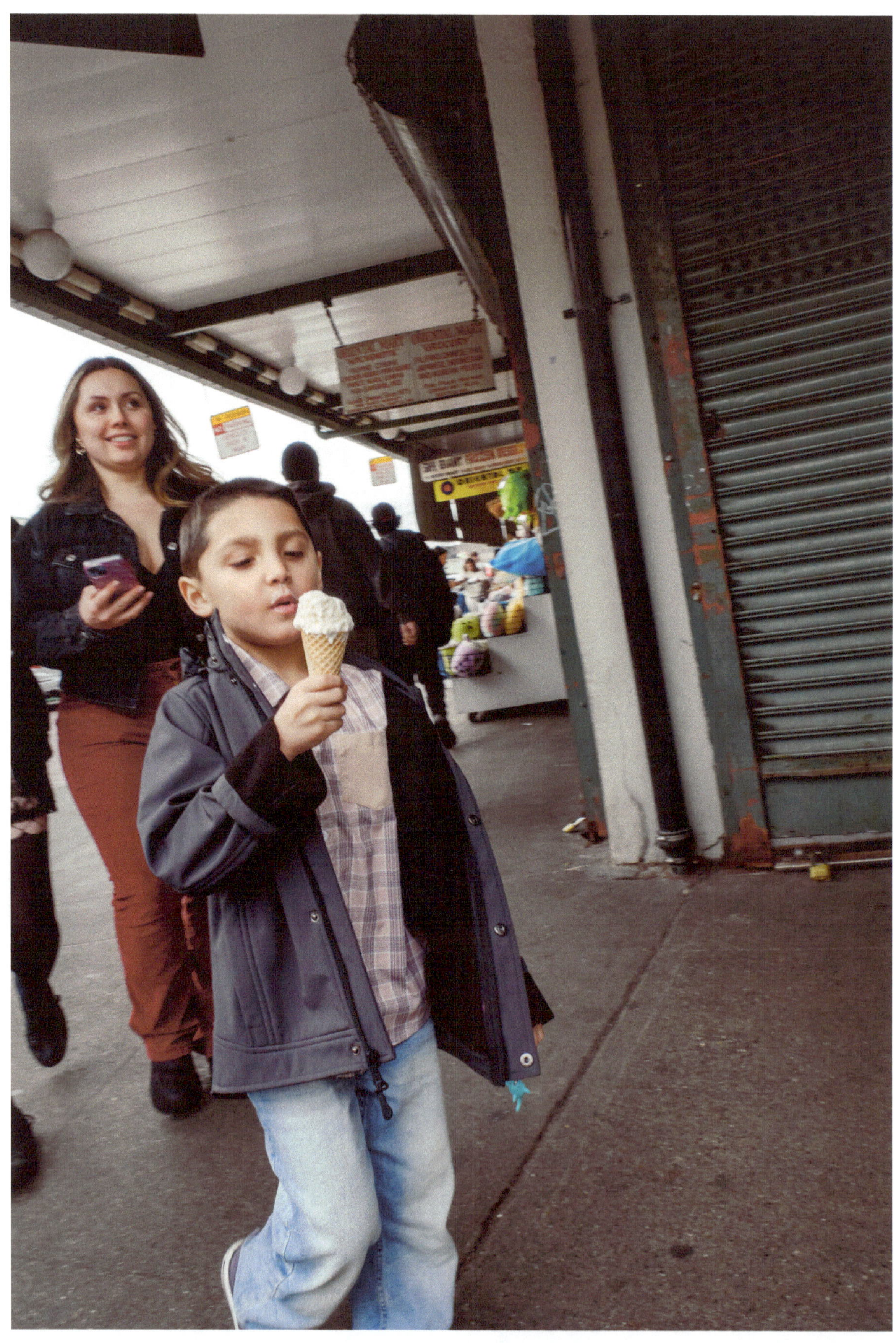

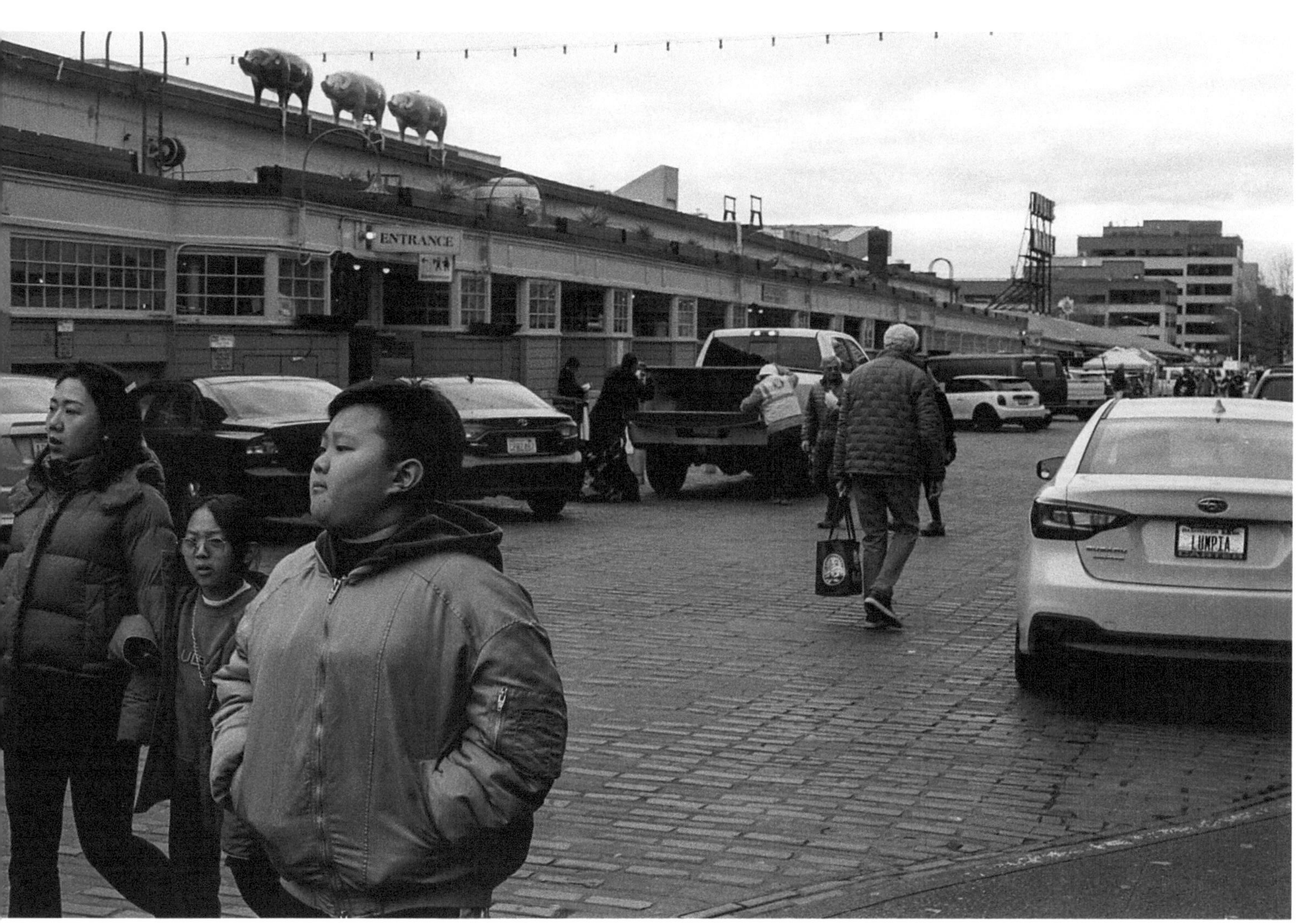

ENTRANCE
LUMPIA

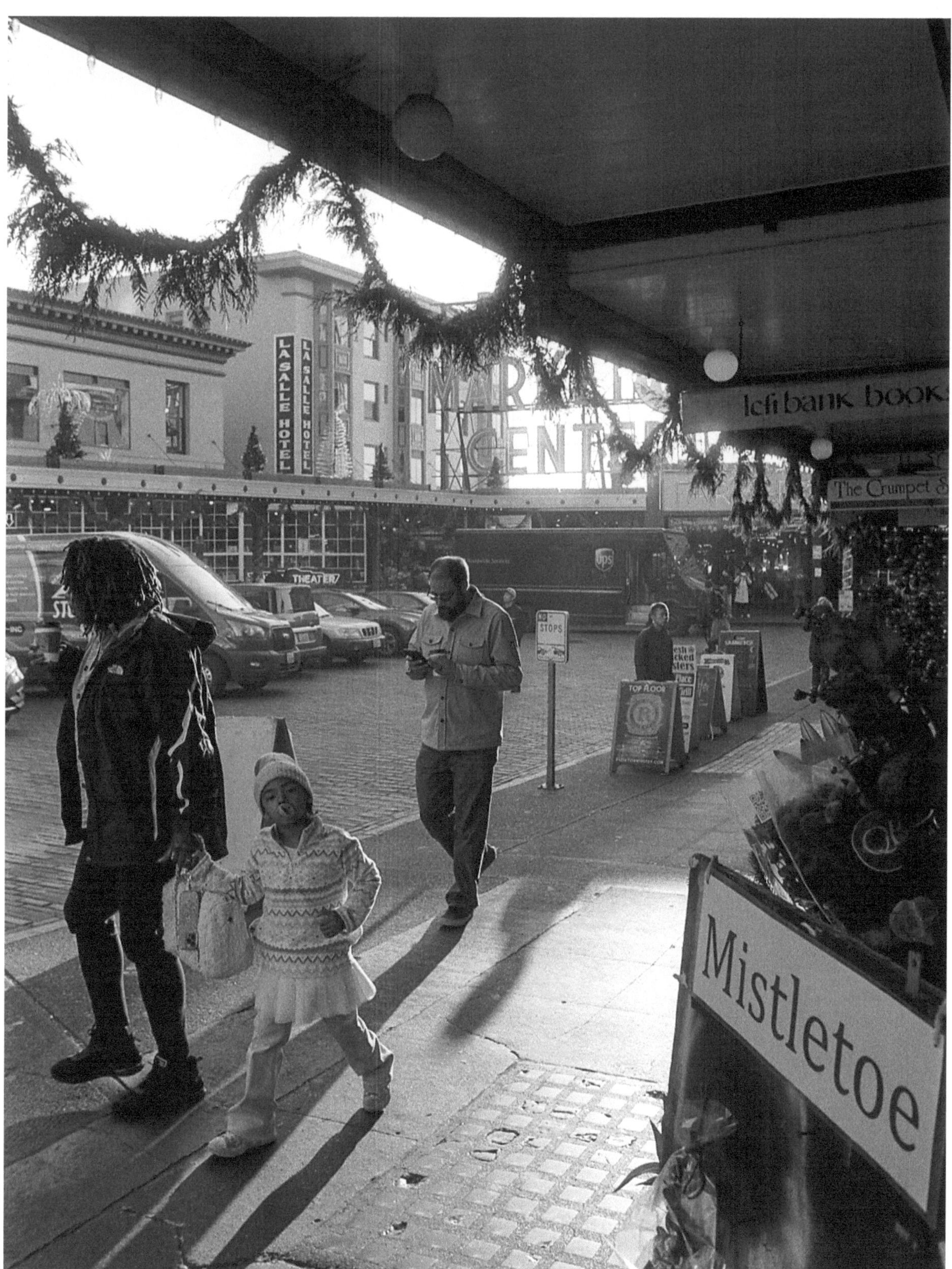

LA SALLE HOTEL
LA SALLE HOTEL
MAR
CENT
left bank books
The Crumpet
THEATER7
UPS
NO
STOPS
TOP FLOOR
Mistletoe

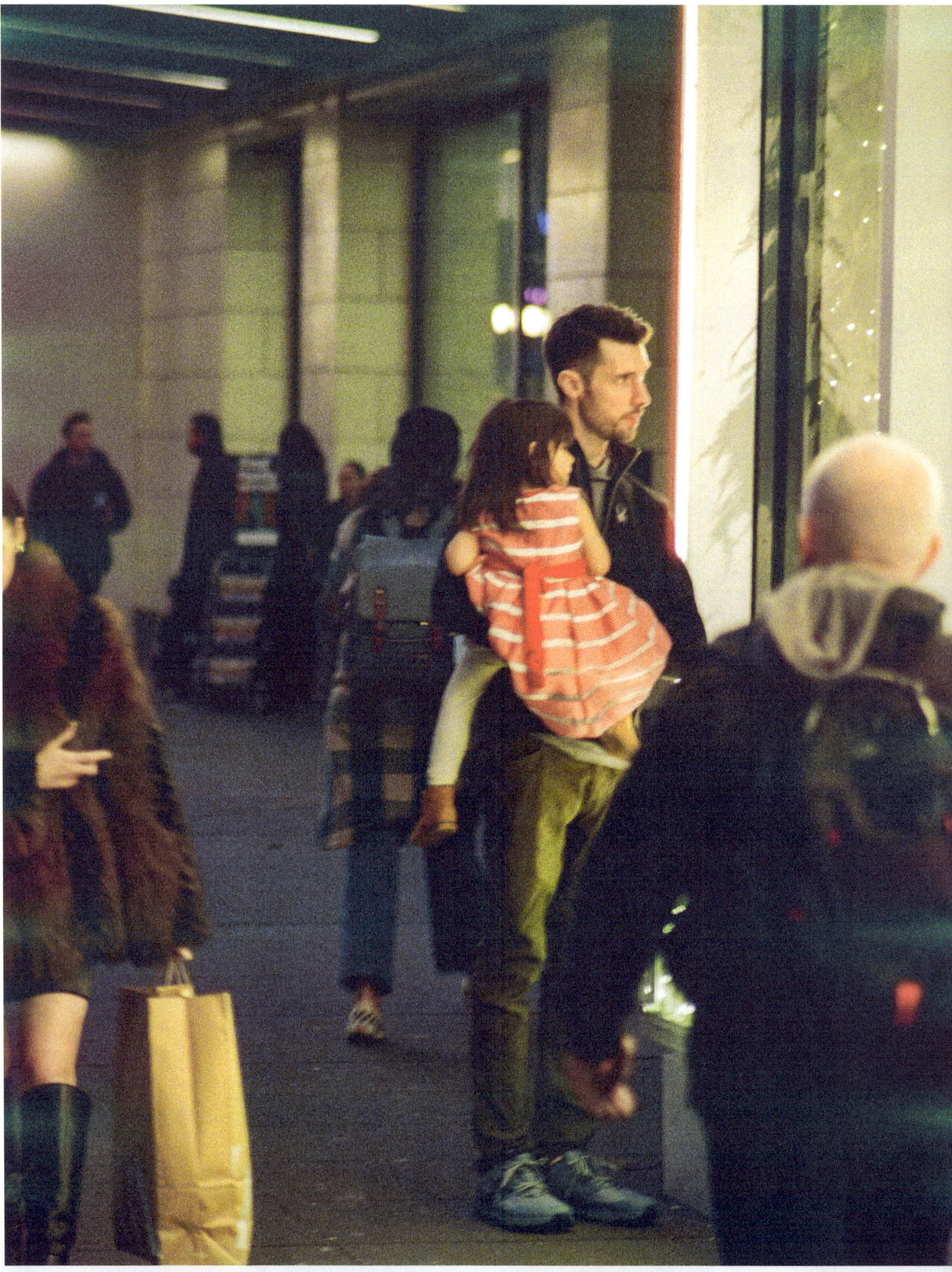

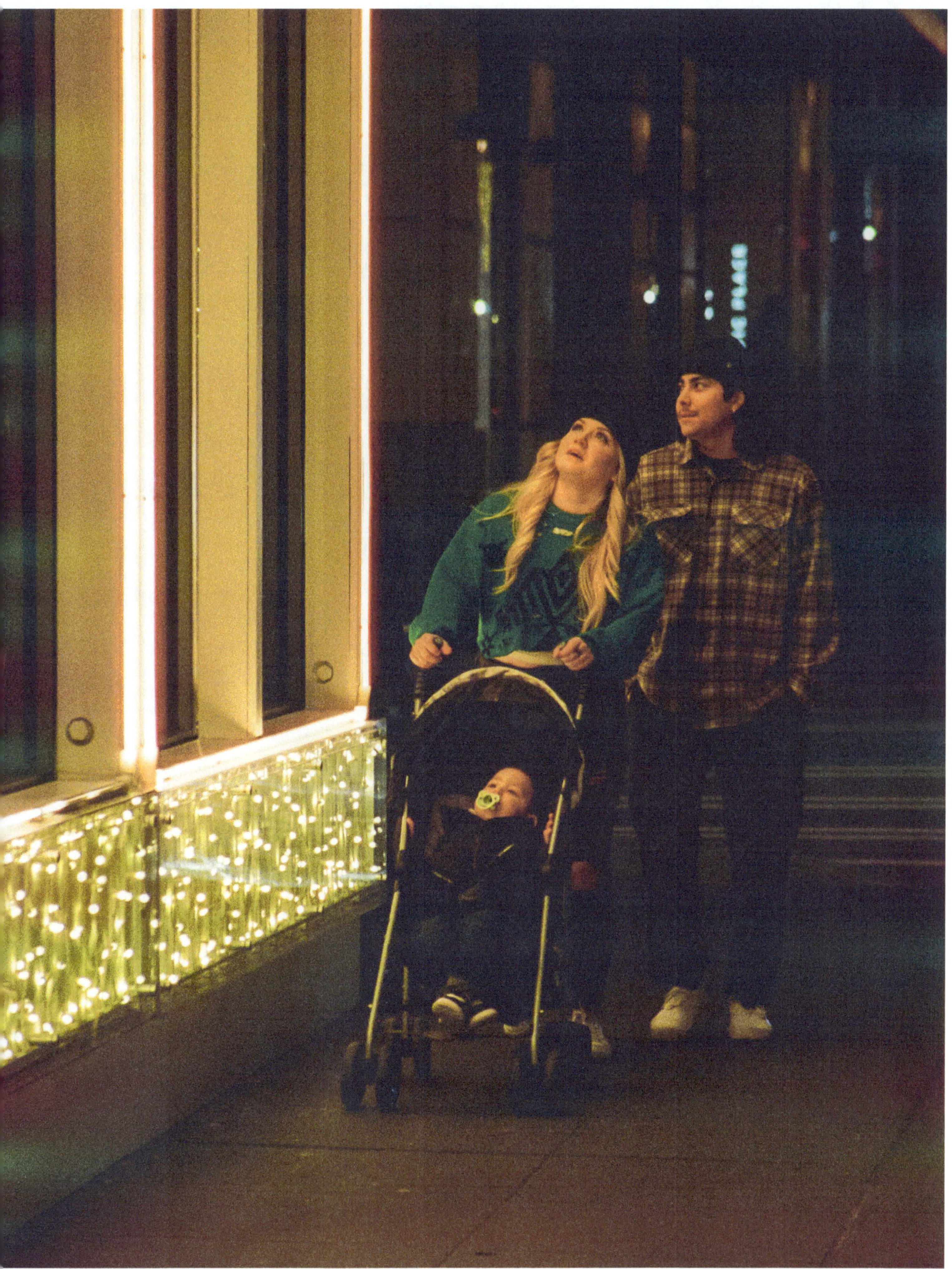

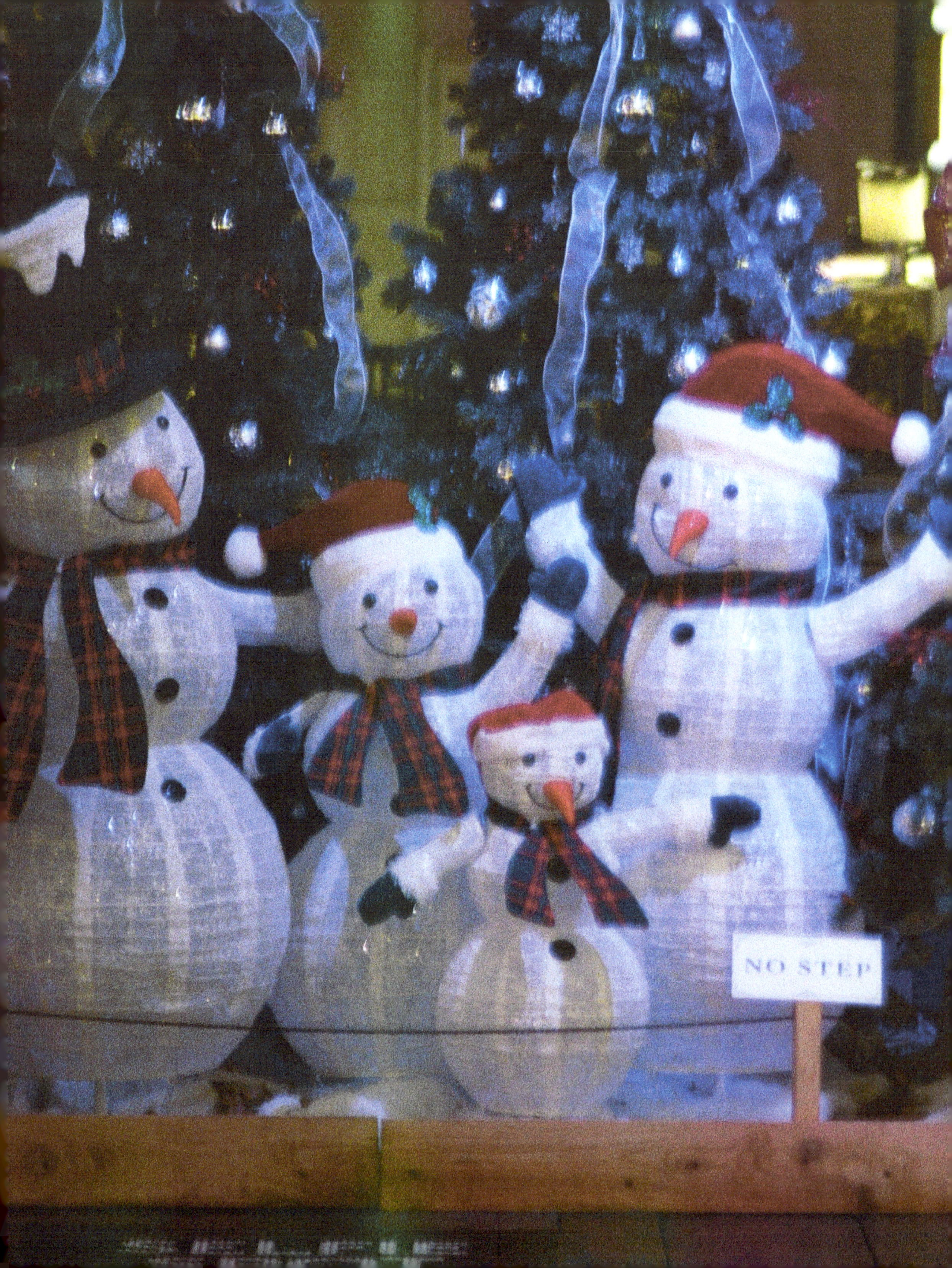
NO STEP

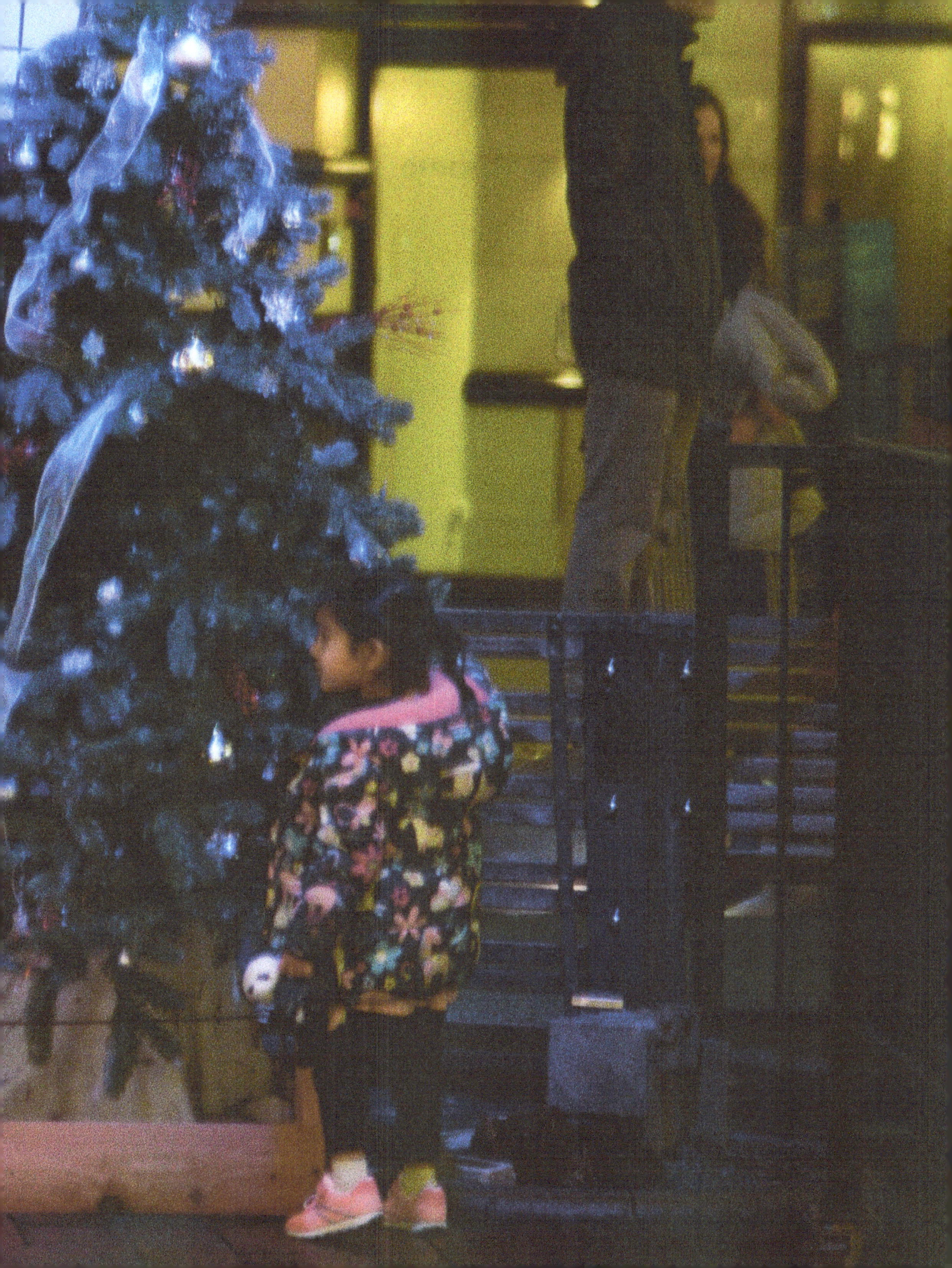

-30-

Enjoyed this book? Consider gifting a copy
to someone you know who'll like it.
Purchasing information available at
mudflappress.com/opc

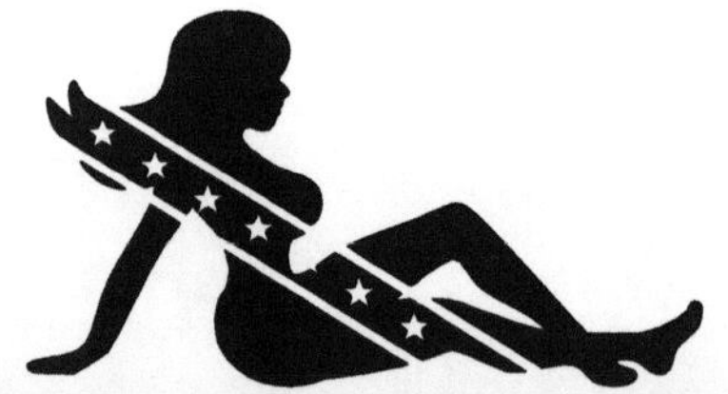

About the author

Ben LoPinto is a photographer, author, and expert communicator who spent most of his life on the East Coast before moving to Seattle in the mid-2010s. He graduated summa cum laude from Washington State University in 2023. *Other People's Children* is his debut photo book.

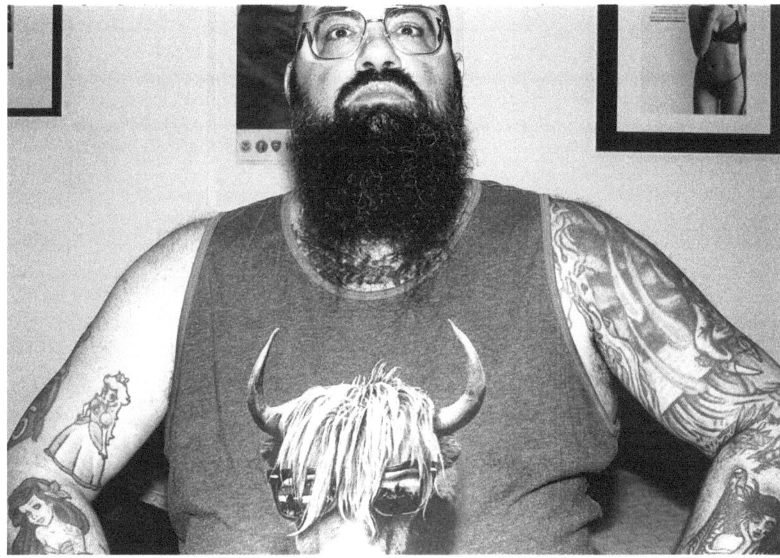

Readers can reach the author at @mudflapgirls on most socials, or on the web at mudflapgirls.org.

www.ingramcontent.com/pod-product-compliance
Lightning Source LLC
Chambersburg PA
CBHW041600110726
48005CB00002B/231